10

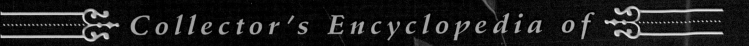

Collector's Encyclopedia of

AMERICAN DINNERWARE

SECOND EDITION

Identification and Values

Jo Cunningham

COLLECTOR BOOKS

A Division of Schroeder Publishing Co., Inc.

Front cover: Middle left: Covered casserole marked "Ohio." The Ohio Pottery Company was a forerunner of The Fraunfelter China Company. **Middle right:** Knowles, Taylor & Knowles biscuit jar. **Bottom left:** Crooksville China plate circa 1950s. **Bottom right:** Leigh China teapot. **Top:** A hard-to-find, three-toed rabbit cotton dispenser made by Southern Potteries (Blue Ridge in its transition phase in the late 1930s).

Back cover: Harker Red Apple kitchen pieces: fork, server, spoon, and rolling pin. Harker Rooster plate. Paden City jug.

Cover design: Beth Summers
Book design: Kelly Dowdy

COLLECTOR BOOKS
P.O. Box 3009
Paducah, Kentucky 42002-3009

www.collectorbooks.com

Copyright © 2005 Jo Cunningham

The current values in this book should be used only as a guide. They are not intended to set prices, which vary from one section of the country to another. Auction prices as well as dealer prices vary greatly and are affected by condition as well as demand. Neither the author nor the publisher assumes responsibility for any losses that might be incurred as a result of consulting this guide.

Searching For A Publisher?

We are always looking for people knowledgeable within their fields. If you feel that there is a real need for a book on your collectible subject and have a large comprehensive collection, contact Collector Books.

Contents

Dedication

The Collector's Encyclopedia of American Dinnerware, Second Edition, is respectfully dedicated to all of the men and women who labored in the American pottery industry and to all of those who treasure the fruits of their labor — and to the memory of Ann Kerr: my encourager, my mentor, and my dearest friend.

Acknowledgments

Many of the contributors to the first book are no longer with us. My memories of those special people will always remain with me. I will always be thankful for their help, their encouragement, and support. They were truly a huge part in the success of this book.

Again, I need to thank my family who has put up with dishes, phone calls, research, trips, and many other things that have taken time away from them over the last 25 plus years. I want to thank them also for allowing and encouraging me to do what I love to do, play with my dishes.

Most of the pieces shown in the book are from my own collection of American dinnerware but many friends supplemented by sharing pieces to be photographed. The following people loaned pieces to be photographed for the original book: B.A. Wellman, Greg Ciccolo, John Moses, Bill Stratton, Bud and Evelyn Rhoades, Harold Shaw, Betty and Jim Cooper, Frank and Norma Hudson, Phyllis Bess, Mark Schliessmann, and Lee Wagner.

Information and/or pieces were provided by Mrs. William H. Blair, Mrs. Howard Blair, Louise Wommack, Jay Block, Al Fridley, Maxine Nelson, John Moses, B.A. Wellman, Allen Kleinbeck, Rex Cunningham, Robert Boyce, John T. Hall, Charles Doll, Phyllis Bess, Ed Carson, Chester Wardeska, Don Hoffmann, Bette Cooper, Eva Zeisel, William Gates, Donna Johnson, Pat Kerr, Hassell, LaVon and Liberty Bell, and Joniece Frank.

I could not have produced this second edition without the help and thoughtfulness of so many. John Austin, William and Donna Gray, Jerry Lefever, Ralph Palmieri, Michael Rechel, Becky Robbins, Darlene Nossaman, Howard and Linda Richards, and Marden and Marie Blackledge have shared pictures, pricing, and lots of encouragement for my projects. Thank you all!

About the Author

Jo Cunningham resides in Springfield, Missouri, with her family. She has been active in collecting for many years and is a member of several national organizations pertaining to collecting. You are welcome to write Jo but if you require an answer, you must enclose a self-addressed, stamped envelope: Jo Cunningham, 535 E. Normal, Springfield, MO 65807.

Introduction

Much has happened in the 22 years this book has been in print. When I did the research for *The Collector's Encyclopedia of American Dinnerware* in the late 1970s, it was very difficult to find pottery information. I called historical societies, libraries, potteries, and talked to pottery workers and pottery management. My husband Wayne and I visited some of the potteries and my search led me to a library in Ohio that had pottery trade journals stored. My dear friend, Ann Kerr, met me at the library and we spent two or three days looking through the journals and inserting dimes for copies that have since faded away to nothing. Now all researchers have to do is look up the name of a pottery on the Internet and with the click of a mouse find lots of information (or possible mis-information.)

As I said in the first edition of the dinnerware book, that "was only a beginning." Now there are many excellent books on several of the major American dinnerware producers. I have also learned over the years that it is not possible to learn everything we as collectors want to know about the American dinnerware industry, but we have more information available now than ever before. For all of the new books and great dinnerware information I am truly grateful.

The most important information collectors of American dinnerware need to know is the dinnerware shapes. Potteries named or gave numbers to their shapes for identification purposes. Decals were added to these shapes for decoration and generally the decals were given numbers rather than names. Most of the time, but not always, the name used is the company's shape name, not the pattern name. Due to the many thousands of decals used by so many different companies, it is often not possible to name the patterns. Decals were not exclusive (unless the company's art director designed the decoration) so it is quite likely to find the same decoration on different shapes from the same company or pieces made by different companies. This may explain why your particular pattern is not in this book.

Pricing

The prices listed here are a guide only. They are not intended to be the final word but are to be used as a general idea or guide to pricing. The prices have been gathered from antique malls, collectors, the Internet, and personal knowledge. Prices are for each piece and are intended for mint condition pieces only. Pieces pictured that are less than perfect will be priced accordingly.

Another thing that has happened over the years with the Internet is that some items we used to consider to be extremely rare are no longer rare. This is due to the large number of people selling and the availability of the items. There really is no market for less than perfect items unless an item is extremely rare or one-of-a-kind. The exception to that rule would be if you are a craftsperson working on mosaics made from broken dinnerware.

I believe that pricing is each collector's responsibility based on their income and desire to own a particular piece of dinnerware. This is especially true on the Internet auctions when you see an item fail to get a bid at one site and at another site an identical item will sell for much more than it should. That's the nature of auctions. Pricing is personal, so once again the prices given in this book are only a guide, not the last word.

The American Pottery Industry: A Brief History

Authorities have not been able to agree on an exact date or site of the first American-made pottery. They do generally agree, however, on the mid-1600s and the New York, New Jersey area. It has been proven that several potteries were in business by the mid-1700s.

Of more importance to us is the East Liverpool, Ohio, area as the beginning of the dinnerware industry as we know it.

James Bennett came to America in 1834 at the age of 22. Early reports say he went to Jersey City and worked at a pottery as a packer. He left Jersey City in 1837 for Troy, Indiana, and after a year or so found himself on a steamboat where a chance meeting with a gentleman from East Liverpool convinced him of the rich clay deposits in the East Liverpool area — or so the story goes.

Bennett started to work on his pottery in the fall of 1839 and the first kiln was drawn in 1840. He was backed to some degree by Benjamin Harker, another important pioneer in the pottery industry. Isaac Knowles became the first crockery salesman, buying two crates and selling it down the river. Mr. Bennett left the area in 1844 but by this time Benjamin Harker was in the pottery business and no doubt news of the clay deposits brought other potters to the area. These early potteries produced yellow ware, and white ware was not developed until 1879 when Harker, Knowles and Laughlin developed white ware at about the same time. From this chance visit by James Bennett, the East Liverpool area evolved into the pottery manufacturing center of the United States.

Early white ware was not considered to be as good as English ware and backstamps gave the impression that American-made white ware was English made. Homer Laughlin is credited with using the American eagle with the British lion on its back, on what we now know to be the first distinctive American backstamp.

The development of white ware created a need for independent decorating shops and early ware was decorated in these shops. Other companies soon cropped up, filling the potteries' needs for machinery, saggers, pins, and any clay products needed.

Many potteries were destroyed by floods and fires only to rebuild and go under in the Depression years. In looking back, it seems to me that the 1940s were the most active years for those manufacturers who had survived. The American public was buying American products. By the mid- to late 1950s it was over for many potteries that had remained. Plastics and the return of imports were obstacles too large to overcome. In the course of 100 years from James Bennett's first kiln drawn in 1840, the great American pottery industry struggled, fought, and overcame floods and fires to reach the very heights of success, only to have the doors of failure end their struggle in the 1950s. At this time only a few pottery companies remain, and little American-made dinnerware is available to the American consumer. Institutional ware makes up the major portion of the wares produced by existing potteries.

How Dinnerware Is Made

A piece of dinnerware has its beginning in the clay shop. All of the ingredients are carefully measured, mixed, and a thin paste called "slip" is made by the addition of water to the dry ingredients. The slip then goes through a sieve and an electromagnet removes all foreign particles. Excess liquid is removed and the clay comes out in a round flat pie crust shape. It then moves to the pug mill. The pug mill squeezes out air bubbles and converts "pie crusts" into fat heavy rolls.

Throwing, casting, and jiggering are the three methods of shaping clay. A ball of clay is "thrown" on the center of a horizontal wheel and water is used as a lubricant to the worker's hands. Jiggering machines were developed to speed the shaping.

Automatic cup forming on Cupmaster jigger. Anchor Hocking, 1980.

Casting is achieved by pouring the slip into plaster of paris molds and allowing it to stand long enough for the plaster to absorb sufficient water. The clay forms a wall of pre-determined thickness inside the mold. Excess slip is poured off and the piece can be removed.

All hollow-ware (or holloware) is made in this manner. Pre-cast handles are pressed into place with slip and the "green-ware" is dried. The soft dishes are racked in rough tile baskets that move by conveyor through the kiln. The bisque, or "biscuits," move to the glazing department and then to another firing. Some ware is decorated before glazing.

The decalomanias are held to a piece by varnish and the paper backing soaked off with water. Delicate presses could press designs with soft rubber engravings. Automatic liners make lines. Final firing burns off the varnish and oil in the paint or decalomanias and the bright colors of dinnerware emerge.

Inspectors cull out all along the line pieces failing to meet specifications. Some pieces not making it are dropped and broken in a large bin by the inspector. A final inspection is made before the pieces are shipped.

The backstamp is just what the name implies. A rubber stamp with the company's name or line name is used on the back of the pieces. Some companies used a date and other marks might signify a worker or factory location. Mr. Doll of the Mt. Clemens operation tells us that after 1938 none of their wares were marked due to the volume of their production.

It will be impossible to definitely identify all ware. All potteries sold seconds, thirds, and even firsts to different jobbers. It is conceivable that the same blanks were sold to several different jobbers or decorators who decorated the ware and stamped it with their own backstamp. Potteries also sold their ware to other potteries and it is not uncommon to find two pottery names on the back of one piece.

From *On American Dinnerware,* by Franklin Ullrey.

Newly formed and dried flatware is automatically removed from quadramatic jigger by use of suction. Anchor Hocking, 1980.

Brushes remove dirt from bisque ware before glaze is applied. Anchor Hocking, 1980.

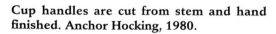

Cup handles are cut from stem and hand finished. Anchor Hocking, 1980.

Handle finishing. Mold marks are smoothed and finished to fit contour of cup. Anchor Hocking, 1980.

Underglaze stamp decorations are applied by machine, one color at a time. (pattern is Currier & Ives) Anchor Hocking, 1980.

Hand application of mug handles. Anchor Hocking, 1980.

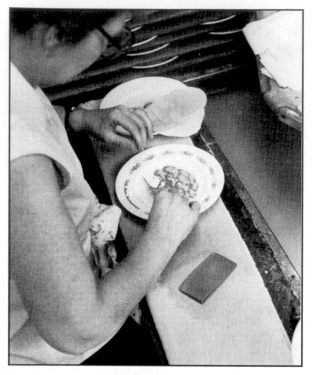

Overglaze decal being applied by hand. Special plate is for Avon Products. Anchor Hocking, 1980.

Automatic cup lining machine. Anchor Hocking, 1980.

Looking into firebox of bisque kiln. Temperature inside is 2,300 degrees. Anchor Hocking, 1980.

Backstamps

This is not a book of marks and some marks shown in this book are enlarged for your convenience. You will find many more marks used by these companies and you are invited to share unlisted marks by sending a sketch or copy to the author. This will help with identification in future books about the American pottery industry. Remember when writing, a self-addressed, stamped envelope is an absolute must if you want a reply.

You will find a variety of backstamps shown. Most are a design or company logo. Some are in raised lettering like Cronin's Bake Oven. Some are incised or cut in the clay before it is hardened and some are as colorful as a peacock, which is exactly what was used on some of the Homer Laughlin Wells lines.

Sometimes the name on the bottom of a piece will be the pattern name but more times than not it is the shape name. There are approximately 150 different patterns on the Virginia Rose blank by Homer Laughlin and they all say Virginia Rose.

One can generally pick a production date out of the numbers on the back of a piece. Numbers can also be a code for factory location and at times provide information known only to the company. It doesn't take long for a dinnerware collector to become a confirmed "backstamp checker." Even though I know the pattern I still feel compelled to double check. My family is somewhat appalled by my habit, especially when visiting or eating out. I soon developed a fast rule for dining out and that is to "backstamp check" before being served or after finishing your meal.

Mr. Robert Boyce, formerly of the Harker operation, told me that backstamps did not have the significance that collectors attach to them. He also tells us a new backstamp was often used to promote some new pattern or line.

Designers

In the late 1930s and 1940s it was popular for dinnerware makers to contract with designers for a special shape or line. This idea carried over into the 1950s but later it is believed the major remaining potteries had their own in-house art department and designers. Some names you will hear associated with American dinnerware are: Eva Zeisel, Russel Wright, Charles Murphy, Ben Seibel, Belle Kogan, Sascha Brastoff, Viktor Schreckengost, Don Schreckengost, Simon Slobodkin, Walter Teague, and J. Palin Thorley.

Eva Zeisel began designing in 1925. She designed aluminum ware, metal-craft frames, and cosmetic lines. An innovator of new shapes, she designed a line of china for Castleton, Red Wing, Butler Brothers, Hall China, and Western Stoneware. Mrs. Zeisel taught at Pratt Institute and was a well-known lecturer on functional design. Mrs. Zeisel came to the United States in 1938.

Russel Wright could well be called the father of American modern design. Mr. Wright created a whole new concept, not only in dinnerware, but in functional furniture, silverware, radios, and lawn furniture.

Russel Wright's American Modern dinnerware was introduced to the trade in 1938 and to the public in 1939. American Modern was made by the Steubenville Pottery in Steubenville, Ohio. Russel Wright designed a Plus Pottery line for Justin Tharaud, dinnerware for Tharaud, Steubenville, Harker, Sterling, and Iroquois. He designed furniture, plastic dinnerware, stainless items, and much more.

Charles Murphy was a graduate of the Cleveland School of Art. He went to Red Wing, Minnesota, to design for Red Wing in the 1940s, from the East Liverpool, Ohio, area. Charles Murphy designed for the Stetson Company for a brief period of time in the 1950s.

Ben Seibel designed Raymor for Roseville, Contempura for Steubenville, and Mr. Seibel's most recent design for American dinnerware was for the Haeger Pottery, Dundee, Illinois.

Belle Kogan was educated at Pratt Institute, Winold Reiss Studios, and the Rhode Island School for Design. She studied in Europe in 1930 and 1931. She designed pottery, glass, plastics, wood, and silver, and also designed clocks and electrical appliances.

Sascha Brastoff designed mostly for California Potteries but created several patterns for Winfield China.

Viktor Schreckengost was a native of Sebring, Ohio. His parents came to Sebring from Pennsylvania where their family had long been potters. Viktor Schreckengost was a design instructor at the Cleveland School of Art and designed glass, stoves, pen sets, enamel furniture, and many other items. By 1934 his work had been exhibited at the Metropolitan Museum, Pennsylvania Museum, Akron Art Institute, Chicago Art Institute, and the Syracuse Museum. He became chief designer for Limoges China Company in about 1938 and designed two new shapes, Americana and Diana. These shapes were decorated in many different ways and colors: Smoke, Coronet, Betsy Rose, Flame, Evening Star Esquire, Penthouse, Pueblo, Crocus Symphony, and Hollywood. Fredrick Rhead called Viktor's Limoges shapes "... the most outstanding creative development by any American potter within the past year" (1934). Viktor Schreckengost studied in Vienna and then studied the people and architecture in Russia and Poland. He divided his time between being instructor at the Cleveland School of Art and serving as an assistant to Guy R. Cowan. Schreckengost later designed for Salem China, Salem, Ohio.

Don Schreckengost, brother of Viktor, designed for Homer Laughlin and the Hall China Company.

Simon Slobodkin designed for W. S. George and others. Walter Teague designed Conversation line for Taylor, Smith & Taylor. J. Palin Thorley designed the "E" line for Sears and Castle and Dogwood for Taylor, Smith & Taylor.

This is not a complete list of designers nor is it a complete list of their works. Most designed not only dinnerware but many other items. I'm sure there will be much more written about these great artists who contributed so much to the great American pottery industry.

Advertising Pieces

Hall China Old Crow punch bowl with cups and ladle. This particular set was given by National Distillers to bar owners on the opening of their new establishments in the 1950s.

Advertising pieces of all kinds have long been popular with collectors. Ad pieces were given away by a variety of businesses over the years. Groceries, furniture stores, cleaners, service stations, and the potteries themselves gave away ashtrays, plates, children's pieces, mugs, and like items to their customers.

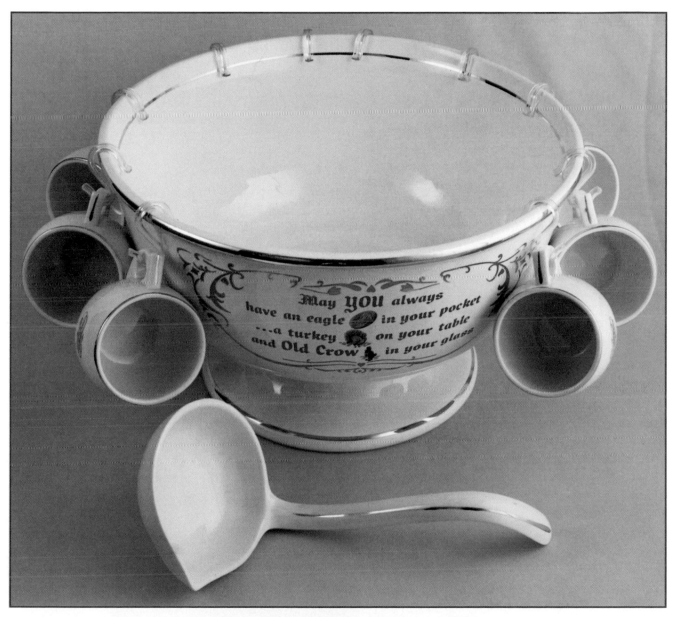

Old Crow punch set, complete. $190.00 – 200.00.

Page 15

Row 1: Order of Eastern Star cup, $2.00 – 3.00; State souvenir cup, $2.00 – 3.00; Toots Shor Hall China ashtray, $20.00 – 25.00; Lake Tower Inn ashtray, $4.00 – 6.00; The Contessa West advertising ashtray, $4.00 – 6.00.

Row 2: Child's plate, maker unknown, advertising on back, $20.00 – 25.00; child's plate, advertising on back, $20.00 – 25.00; child's bowl, Continental Kilns, advertising on back, $15.00 – 20.00; Small Harker plate, advertising on back, $15.00 – 20.00.

Row 3: Plate, Thompson China Company, advertising on back, $15.00 – 20.00; Hall China Irish coffee mug, Tri-state Pottery Festival, $10.00 – 15.00; Hall China Irish coffee mug, MacAuthur Insurance, $8.00 – 10.00; pink rose egg plate, decorated by the Sabin Company, $15.00 – 20.00.

Row 4: Furniture company advertising plate, Homer Laughlin, $20.00 – 25.00; Crosley dishwasher advertising plate, $15.00 – 18.00; 1967 Harker Postmaster's Convention commemorative plate on the Heritage shape, $3.00 – 5.00.

My own personal favorite advertising piece is shown below. A Hall China #1273 Irish Coffee mug, white with black lettering and base commemorating the annual Glaze American Pottery Earthenware and China Show and Sale held in Springfield, Illinois, the fourth weekend in September.

Hall China #1273 Irish coffee mug advertising "the glaze" annual American Pottery Earthenware & China shows. $10.00 – 15.00.

Page 17

Row 1: Harker Mr. Zip Code pencil holder, $15.00 – 20.00; Harker 1920s Gem shape creamer, grocery store giveaway, $15.00 – 17.00; Taylor, Smith & Taylor's Silhouette cup advertising Hellick's coffee, $10.00 – 15.00; early Harker scenic plate, grocery advertising on back, $10.00 – 12.00; Steubenville small platter/gravy liner with advertising on back, "souvenir of KENJ.," $20.00 – 25.00.

Row 2: Harker Kelvinator covered refrigerator jug, $15.00 – 25.00; Harker Kelvinator stack set, complete, $25.00 – 30.00; Harker Kelvinator covered bowl, $20.00 – 75.00; Harker Kelvinator rolling pin, $75.00.

Row 3: Hall China Sanka coffee set: mug, $6.00 – 8.00; pot, $15.00 – 20.00; mug, $6.00 – 8.00; Homer Laughlin Bell Savings and Loan Sit 'N Sip set, includes mug and coaster, $15.00 – 18.00.

Row 4: Crown plate, $20.00 – 25.00; Harker Cherry pitcher, $55.00 – 65.00; Crown plate, $20.00 – 25.00. All grocery store giveaways. The name of the business may be found on the front, back, or bottom of the piece.

I was somewhat surprised to learn that some of the mugs in the Sanka set were made in Japan. The Hall China Sanka mug has an ivory glaze, as compared to the white glaze on the "made in Japan." There are slight differences in color and placement of decals, slight differences in the handles, and, of course, differences in the markings. The Hall China mug is marked, "made expressly for Sanka Brand Decaffeinated Coffee, furnished by Minners and Co., Inc., Hall China." The other mug is marked, "made expressly for Sanka® Brand De-Caffeinated Coffee, Made in Japan."

A variety of advertising ashtrays made by The Harker Company, Chester, West Virginia. $2.00 – 4.00 each.

Row 1: Reserved for a Wonderful Guy; King Cole; D FINE FOODS.

Row 2: Be American; Harker China Company; Waterford Park.

Row 3: Sunnyland's Fine Meats; Fontainebleau; Tennessee.

Row 1: Edwin M. Knowles Yorktown plate, $20.00 – 25.00; W. C. Bunting Co. server, $15.00 – 20.00; grocery store plate, maker unknown, $25.00 – 30.00.

Row 2: Harker plate Sandner's Dry Goods; Notions plate, Men's clothing, 1930, $15.00 – 18.00; Homer Laughlin Palestine Theatre plate on Century shape, $45.00 – 50.00; Limoges China Company ashtray, $35.00 – 40.00; Trenton Potteries ashtray, $15.00 – 20.00.

Row 3: Crown Pottery plate, Best Wishes 1931, $20.00 – 25.00; Syracuse China plate, $30.00 – 35.00; early 1900s plate made by the McNicol Company, East Liverpool, Ohio, $15.00 – 20.00.

American Chinaware Corporation

An article appearing in the *Glass and Crockery Journal*, Vol. 107, 1929, lists the following companies as being part of the American Chinaware Corporation: The Carrollton China Company, Carrollton, Ohio; Knowles, Taylor, Knowles, East Liverpool, Ohio; National China Company, Salineville, Ohio; Pope Gosser China Company, Coshocton, Ohio; Saxon China Company, Sebring, Ohio; E. H. Sebring China, Sebring, Ohio; Smith-Phillips, East Liverpool, Ohio; and Strong Manufacturing Company, Sebring, Ohio. Strong Manufacturing was an enamelware operation.

The Ohio Secretary of State could find no officers listed for the corporation. An article in a 1929 *Glass and Crockery Journal* announces the establishment of the American Chinaware Corporation "in Chicago under the supervision of Ray Cliff, formerly of Sebring." The new home offices and central location was to be the Terminal Tower Building in Cleveland, Ohio.

Also, from a 1929 and *Glass Crockery Journal*, another important announcement was the hiring of Joseph Thorley as designer and stylist for American Chinaware Corporation. Thorley came from a long line of Staffordshire "artists, sculptors and potters." His background before coming to America was impressive. Thorley had studied at the "College of Art, Stoke on Trent, and at the Staffordshire College of Science." He was a lecturer and teacher and served his ceramic apprenticeship at Josia Wedgwood Pottery. He came to America permanently in 1927. Securing such talent was quite a coup for the A.C.C. but even their well-laid plans and J. Thorley could not overcome the stock market crash of 1929.

Information provided by the office of the Ohio Secretary of State shows that American Chinaware Corporation was formed November 23, 1928, and cancelled November 15, 1932. The principal location was listed as Beechwood Village, Ohio. No officers were listed either with the Secretary of State office or the Ohio Taxation Bureau.

Parent company of the American Chinaware Corporation was Knowles, Taylor & Knowles. American Chinaware Corporation used the K. T. and K. plants in East Liverpool, Ohio, from 1929 to 1931.

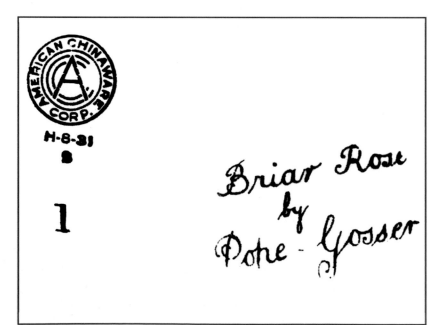

1931 backstamp from a Pope-Gosser Briar Rose shape plate that also included American Chinaware Corporation backstamp.

Bennington Potters

Bennington Potters was founded about 1949 in Bennington, Vermont, by David Gil. Mr. Gil is a graduate of Alfred University and considered to be a leader in the contemporary craft movement.

Bennington Potters is located on the site of the Norton Factory, founded in 1794. Early Bennington pieces are sought after by collectors.

Bennington Potters made Honeycomb for The Block China Company in 1979. It was available in two deep tone colors, Blueberry and Brown Sugar.

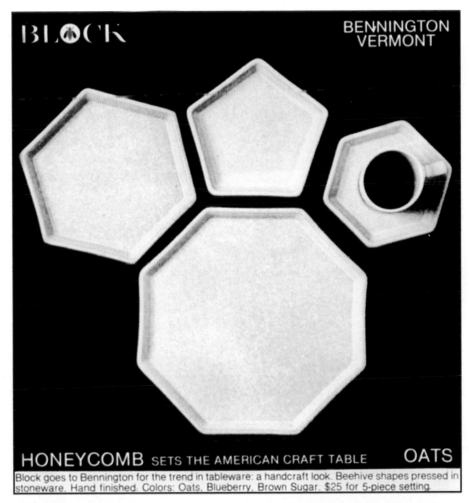

A recent Honeycomb sales brochure. Bennington Potters made this shape for Block China Company.

FAMOUS BENNINGTON DINNERWARE — Ovenproof and dishwasher safe. (From top, reading left to right)

D/1630	10 Cup Coffee Pot, 10¾" high $10.00
D/1639	Mug, 4¾" high, $1.50
D/1682	Large Serving Platter, 16" x 9½" $12.00
D/1648	Serving Platter, 14" x 8½" $7.00
D/1663	Large Bowl, 9" diameter, 3" high $6.00
D/1669	Buffet Plate, 10" diameter $2.50
D/1629	Dinner Plate, 9½" diameter $2.00

D/1628	Luncheon Plate, 8½" diameter $1.80
D/1661	Bread & Butter, 6" diameter $1.00
D/1626	Cup, 2½" high $1.30
D/1627	Saucer, 6" diameter $.90
D/1680	Gravy Boat (t stand), 9" x 5" $6.00
D/1688	Ashtray, 4½" diameter $1.50
D/1635	Creamer, 3½" high $1.50

D/1634	Sugar Bowl, 4½" high $2.00
D/1681	Tray, 5" x 9" $2.00
D/1683	Covered Butter, 8" x 3½" x 1½" high $4.00
D/1667	Fruit Dish, 4½" diameter $1.40
D/1641	Soup/Salad Bowl, 5½" diameter $1.70
D/1660	Salt & Pepper Set, 2½" high $2.50 pr.

All dinnerware is available in: MOUNTAIN BLUE, WHITE, VERMONT GREEN, RUST, TAWNY. (as illustrated by cups and saucers left to right) For information on sets, turn to Page 2.

Front side of an eight-page Bennington Potters sales brochure, 1966 – 1967.

Back side of an eight-page Bennington Potters sales brochure, 1966 – 1967.

Blair Ceramics

Blair Ceramics, Incorporated, was founded in Ozark, Missouri, in 1946 by William Blair. Mr. Blair, an Ohioan, was a modernistic painter turned potter. He was a graduate of the Cleveland School of Art and furthered his art education in Europe. Mr. Blair returned to his native Ohio and eventually became involved with the Purinton Pottery Company.

Mr. Blair let his objections to the basic, round dinnerware shapes be known. He tried to influence some of the Ohio potteries to change the shape of their lines but was rejected.

Mr. Blair had visited the Ozarks earlier and liked the slower pace and, in 1945, moved to southern Missouri and spent the next year in preparations. The plant was opened in 1946 in Ozark, Missouri. A $15,000 kiln was shipped to the plant from West Virginia and during Blair's peak operational period the pottery employed up to 30 workers from the small town of Ozark.

Most Blair pieces are signed, and Blair dinnerware was shipped to all of the then 48 existing states, Hawaii, Cuba, and Canada. Thirty-six hundred pieces were produced weekly during the peak period. Neiman-Marcus and Marshall-Field's were just two of the better known department stores seeking to stock Blair dinnerware.

Blair Ceramics closed in the 1950s. Molds for Blair's oven-proof dinnerware were purchased by a former Blair employee. The former employee tells us she has no future plans for the molds.

Page 25
Row 1: Blair "Rick-Rack" bowl, $15.00 – 20.00; Bamboo covered onion soup bowl, $25.00; Bamboo cup/saucer set, $15.00 – 20.00; Bamboo covered sugar, $18.00 – 20.00.

Row 2: Bamboo 8" square plate, $15.00 – 18.00; Bamboo coffee server (lid missing). If complete, $45.00 – 50.00. As is, $20.00 – 25.00; Bamboo creamer, $20.00 – 25.00.

Row 3: Yellow Plaid dinner serving plate, $45.00 – 50.00.

Row 4: Bamboo square dinner plate, $18.00 – 20.00; Bamboo rectangular plate or server, $15.00 – 18.00.

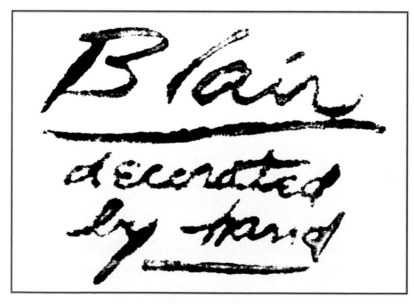

Blair backstamp.

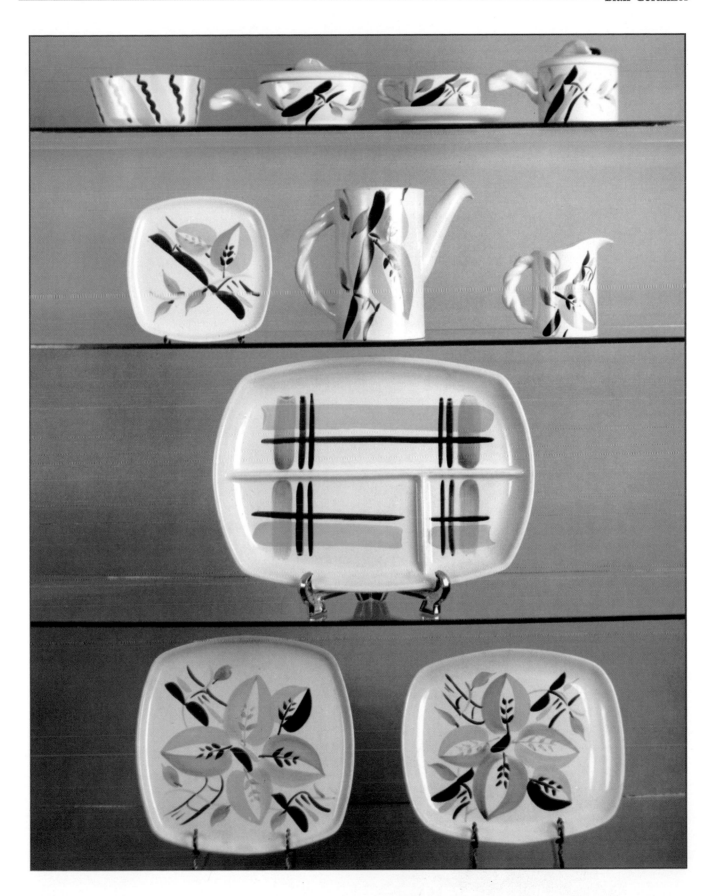

The most popular pattern Blair made, Gay Plaid or Plaid, was made continuously during Blair's brief operational period in Ozark, Missouri. Gay Plaid was nationally distributed to all parts of the United States. The twisted handles and leaf knobs are unique features of Blair ware. All pieces shown on page 27 are Gay Plaid pattern.

Page 27
Row 1: Cup/saucer set, $12.00 – 15.00; covered sugar, $20.00 – 22.00; salt and pepper set, $15.00 – 20.00 set; unusual closed handle cup/saucer set, $15.00 – 20.00.

Row 2: Handled mug, $15.00 – 18.00; creamer, $20.00 – 25.00; milk/utility pitcher, $25.00 – 30.00; tall tumbler, $20.00 – 25.00.

Row 3: Handled triangular soup, $15.00 – 20.00; large water pitcher with ice lip, $50.00 – 60.00; covered soup with lid, $20.00 – 25.00 complete.

Row 4: Dinner plate, $15.00 – 20.00; bowl, $10.00 – 15.00; casserole bowl with handles, $25.00 – 30.00.

Blair Gay Plaid water cooler, 12" high, 30" around middle of cooler, $125.00 – 150.00.

Blair Gay Plaid canister set, complete, $250.00 – 350.00 set.

Rare Primitive Bird pitcher, 10½", $450.00 – 500.00.

Rare Brick saucer, $6.00 – 8.00; Brick syrup jug, $45.00 – 50.00; Brick plate, $16.00 – 18.00.

Page 29

Row 1: All Autumn Leaf. Nut dish, $10.00 – 15.00; bowl, $15.00 – 18.00; cup, $10.00 – 15.00.

Row 2: Bird 6" plate, $15.00 – 20.00; Bird unusual vinegar bottle, needs stopper, $25.00 – 30.00; Bird salt and pepper, $25.00 – 30.00 set; saucer, does not have bird design, $15.00 – 20.00.

Row 3: Bird celery dish, $20.00 – 25.00; Bird dinner plate, $20.00 – 25.00.

Row 4: Bird divided vegetable, $30.00 – 35.00; Bird square plate, $25.00 – 30.00.

Bird, or "Primitive Bird," as it was sometimes called, came later in Blair's Ozarks career. With red base clay for the body, a scraffito bird made for an unusual combination. It is difficult to find the red clay pieces that are not chipped. These are probably the rarest of the Blair pieces. There is also a Brick pattern in the red clay (not shown); the design scratched in the clay gives the appearance of a brick.

Reprint from a 1949 *St. Louis Post-Dispatch Magazine* article.

Block China Company

The Block China Company of New York is important to mention in that it is a distributor and not a manufacturer of dinnerware.

The Block Company was founded by J & I Block in the early 1930s and served as distributor for Cameron Clay Products in Cameron, West Virginia. During the thirties, Block also bought from the Cronin China Company.

Jay L. Block of Block China Company graciously provided us with Block Company history. Mr. Block also provided us with brochures of both Bennington and Hall China that were made for and distributed by Block.

We also now know, through information provided by Mr. Block, that his father, founder of The Block China Company, distributed goods purchased from the Cronin China Company under the Pottery Guild name.

Pottery Guild pieces may be from a variety of makers. "Hostess Ware, handpainted in U. S. A." will be found on some pieces. The Pottery Guild Hostess Ware pieces were plentiful in the late thirties and early forties.

Liberty Hall American Ironstone was made by The Hall China Company for The Block China Company. Liberty Hall was made in Colonial White undecorated.

Martha's Vineyard has a green and grape color Vineleaf border decoration with solid green accessories.

Maine Village has shades of blue on an Early American rustic Village scene, with solid blue accessories.

Mt. Vernon colors are Honey & Brick Red, with a tulip border decoration and solid honey colored accessories.

The following items were made in the mid-1960s in solid colors and Colonial White: cup, 6½" cereal soup, covered sugar, creamer, coffee pot, soup tureen.

The Up-beat collection was made in the mid-1960s by The Hall China Company for The Block China Company. The Up-Beat collection was designed by Gerald Gulatta.

Toccata is described as "an explosion of fantasy flowers in the newest colors: ochre, orange, daffodil, ... with daffodil alone for accent."

Backstamps from Block China Company.

Folk Song is described as "a lively, fresh theme, hand-painted look may be Scandinavian, Mediterranean and is American – Crafts ... blue on white, accent pieces in solid blue."

Impressions pieces
"Sing with color, blue and green that play a bold duet and vibrate together. The color newness, stressed with solid green."

Reprint from a 1966 issue of *China Glass Tablewares*, used by permission.

Block China Impressions plate, $8.00 – 10.00; cup/saucer, $12.00 – 15.00 set.

IMPRESSIONS, one of three patterns in new Up-Beat stackable stoneware dinnerware and coordinated glassware; offered in green and blue with green accessories. Retail: $25 for 45-piece set; in plain white, $20. Block China Company.

LIBERTY HALL
AMERICAN IRONSTONE

LIBERTY HALL is authentic Ironstone, handmade in America by one of our oldest quality tableware factories, The Hall China Company.

The shape, decorations, and colors of LIBERTY HALL are Early Americana. Our Ironstone is dishwasher safe, ovenproof, and chip resistant to give you long years of carefree service.

		List Prices
1.	Dinner Plate 10¾"	$1.95
2.	Salad Plate 7½"	1.55
3.	Bread & Butter 6½"	1.15
4.	Tea Cup	1.30
5.	Tea Saucer	.70
6.	Cereal Soup 6½"*	1.50
7.	Fruit Saucer 6"	1.00
8.	Luncheon Plate 8½"	1.65
9.	Rim Soup 9¼"	1.75
10.	Covered Sugar*	3.25
11.	Creamer	2.50
12.	Coffee Pot	5.50
13.	Round Baker 10¼"	3.00
14.	Platter 13½"	4.35
15.	Platter 17"	4.75
16.	Turkey Platter 19"	6.00
17.	Square Server 10⅛"	3.50
18.	Round Chop Plate 14"	5.00
19.	Soup Tureen*	7.50
20.	Sauceboat Server	5.50

(*) Items are available in Colonial White or Solid Color Treatments Only.

LIBERTY HALL
AMERICAN IRONSTONE

COLONIAL WHITE—*Undecorated with a white traditional ironstone glaze.*

MARTHA'S VINEYARD—*Green and Grape color vineleaf border decoration, solid green accessories.*

MAINE VILLAGE—*Multi shades of blue, Early American rustic village scene, solid blue accessories.*

MT. VERNON—*Honey and Brick Red tulip border decoration, solid honey accessories.*

Martha's Vineyard • Maine Village • Mt. Vernon

Colonial White

Both sides of a Block China "fold top" card.

A step ahead of tomorrow—the Up-Beat Collection by Block. American — definitely: in mood, manner, material. Up-Beat is <u>stoneware</u>, made for Block by the Hall China Company.

Todays young swing shape: smooth, simple, uncluttered. Try stacking Up-Beat. Cup into saucer — solid, firm. Everything fits for easy storage, compact; a today word that's distinctly new in tableware. Designed by Gerald Gulotta. Young Americans have never seen a tableware more its own.

TOCCATA

An explosion of fantasy flowers in the newest colors: ochre, orange, daffodil, . . . with daffodil alone for accent.

FOLK SONG

A lively, fresh theme, hand-painted look may be Scandinavian, Mediterranean, and is American-crafts . . . Blue on white, accent pieces in solid blue.

IMPRESSIONS

Sings with color, blue and green that play a bold duet and vibrate together. The color newness stressed with solid green.

Front of a Block sales brochure.

Inside of a Block sales brochure.

California Potteries

The history of California potteries can be traced back to the Spanish fathers and the early missions. A whole volume or volumes will be needed to cover this vast subject, and we can only briefly touch on it in the space allotted here.

Around 1927, when the use of talc in the body was introduced, so were color glazes on California ware. The natural abundance of some of the raw materials used in dinnerware account for the large number of manufacturers. In 1949 more than half of the dinnerware manufacturers were located in California. California's "Big Five" are listed below:

J. A. Bauer was established in 1909 in Los Angeles, California. Stoneware, flower containers, and gardenlines were his mainstay until 1927 when he used color for kitchen bowls. Bauer's dinnerware line was added a few years later.

Gladding McBean & Company was organized in 1875 as a sewer pipe manufacturer. Gladding McBean purchased Willis Prouty's formula for using talc as a basic ingredient. A ceramic engineer for Gladding McBean improved the Prouty formula and the process became known as "Malinite." Gladding McBean began the pottery manufacturing phase in 1934. Frederic J. Grant was director. The company's Franciscan ware was the first California ware to be marketed in eastern states. Its first dinnerware was El Patio.

Pacific Clay Products Company started making dinnerware in 1932. This company, too, had formerly been a sewer pipe manufacturer. The company's art director was M. J. Lattie, and it used very bright shades of reds, blues, greens, and yellows, and later added pastels.

Vernon Kilns began in 1916 when an Englishman named Paxon used European techniques. A fire destroyed the factory in December 1947, and the plant built to replace it was considered "the most modern ceramic plant in the world." G. Bennison became owner in 1931. Vernon Kilns is famous for its state plates, popular with collectors.

Metlox Poppy Trail Manufacturing Company made tableware, directed by President Willis Prouty (son of the Prouty credited with discovering the talc formula). Controlling interest was sold in 1946 and Metlox introduced its first popular line, California Ivy.

Catalina Pottery is credited with being the first California pottery to use color. Wm. Wrigley, Jr. built a small plant on Catalina Island and products were sold in a small shop on the pier. The company was purchased in 1937 by Gladding McBean & Company, who continued to make the Catalina line until the war years.

Briefly, some other California names you may encounter are:

American Ceramic Products Corporation, made up of La Mirada and Winfield China. Winfield was marketed under "Gabriel" ware in 1949 and became so popular the La Mirada art ware line was dropped.

California Figurine Company, founded by Max Weil (an important name in California ware). He purchased California Art Pottery line in 1945 and changed the name to Max Weil of California. A light new body was developed and Malay Bambu entered the dinnerware field in 1947.

Santa Anita Potteries began about 1939 and had a line of solid color as its first production items. It was purchased by National Silver Company. Flintridge China Company, Pasadena, opened by Hogan and Mason in 1945. M.C. Wentz started with $400.00 in mid-Depression. Wentz later had a Westward Ho line manufactured by Wallace and designed by Till Goodan that was popular.

The pieces pictured are made by Bauer Pottery. They are heavy, durable, and very collectible.

Row 1: Cup and saucer, $20.00 – 25.00; tumbler, Ring pattern, $22.00 – 28.00.

Row 2: Bauer Ring 10" plate, $20.00 – 25.00; mixing/utility bowl, $45.00 – 50.00.

Page 35

Row 1: Metlox Poppy Trail "Rooster" sugar and creamer set, $25.00 – 30.00; Vernon Kilns Organdie small plate, $10.00 – 12.00; Organdie covered casserole, $40.00 – 45.00.

Row 2: Metlox "Rooster" plate, $20.00 – 25.00; Winfield Dragonflower individual ashtray, $4.00 – 6.00; Winfield Dragonflower dinner plate, $10.00 – 12.00.

Row 3: Vernon Kilns coffee jug, $55.00 – 60.00; Tam O'Shanter divided vegetable bowl, $30.00 – 35.00; Homespun tumblers, $20.00 – 25.00 each. Mrs. Nelson tells us there were six different color combinations, each with a different name.

Row 4: Vernon Kilns Mayflower bowl, 1940s to late 1950s, $15.00 – 20.00; Mexican motif plate with Mission Bell backstamp, $25.00 – 30.00; Vernon Kilns cobalt blue bowl, $125.00 – 150.00.

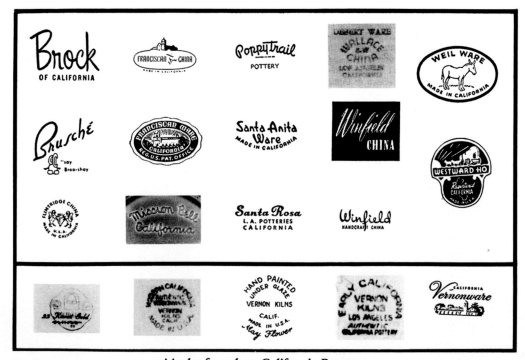

Marks found on California Pottery.

Page 37

Row 1: Orange-red after-dinner cup and saucer, $20.00 – 25.00 set; Vernon Kilns after-dinner creamer and sugar, $15.00 – 20.00 set; Vernon Kilns orange-red cup and saucer, $20.00 – 28.00 set; Vernon Kilns blue cup, $12.00 – 15.00.

Row 2: Franciscan Coronado pitcher, $45.00 – 50.00; salt/pepper, $20.00 – 25.00 set; sugar, lid, creamer, $30.00 – 35.00 set; coffee pot and lid, $60.00 – 65.00.

Row 3: Franciscan Coronado Faststand gravy boat (attached liner), $20.00 – 25.00; plate, $12.00 – 14.00; ¼-lb. covered butter, $30.00 – 35.00; pink swirl plate, $10.00 – 12.00; cream colored bowl, $18.00 – 20.00 (the butter, plate, and bowl may not be Franciscan).

Row 4: Vernon Kilns brown divided plate, 1930s, $12.00 – 15.00; brown cup and saucer, $15.00 – 20.00 set; Franciscan water set, $135.00 – 165.00; tumblers, $15.00 – 20.00 each; pitcher, $60.00 – 65.00.

Franciscan's swirl type pattern was called Coronado; Metlox's swirl is Yorkshire. (See Metlox reprint).

Vernon Kilns Fleur de Lis large plate, $100.00 – 125.00.

COLORS: Gloss Glazes, Vivid Colors: Delphinium Blue, Old Rose, Canary Yellow, Turquoise Blue, Poppy Orange and Rust.

Satin Glazes, Pastel Colors: Opaline Green, Powder Blue, Petal Pink, Pastel Yellow, Satin Turquoise, Peach and Satin Ivory.

YORKSHIRE

DINNERWARE ★ BEVERAGEWARE ★ KITCHENWARE

Pintoria   COLORS: Gloss Glazes, Vivid Colors: Delphinium Blue, Old Rose, Canary Yellow, Turquoise Blue, Poppy Orange and Rust.

Poppytrail   POTTERY by METLOX   Poppytrail

Metlox brochure, circa 1939.

Catalina fish plate, very unusual, no established price.

Canonsburg Pottery Company

The Canonsburg Pottery Company was founded in 1900 by John George, nephew of W. S. George. The plant was first called Canonsburg China Company and produced sanitary and hotel ware.

About 1909, the name was changed to Canonsburg Pottery Company and it then specialized in dinnerware, producing about 25,000 dozen pieces a week.

Steubenville's equipment and molds were sold to Canonsburg Pottery after Steubenville's closing in 1959. Adam Antique and Rose Point, two of Steubenville's popular patterns, were sold into the 1960s under the Steubenville name. A line called Partio was also sold in the 1960s under the Steubenville name, Canonsburg, Pennsylvania.

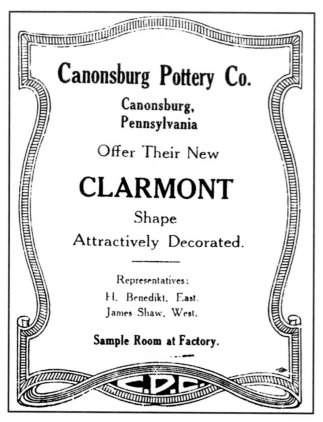

Canonsburg Pottery Co. advertisement, 1920s.

A very early cream pitcher with the Canonsburg China mark. The backstamp dates this piece to circa 1900 – 1909. $12.00 – 15.00.

Canonsburg backstamps.

Caribe-Sterling China Company

The Puerto Rican government built a china facility in San Juan as part of its "Operation Bootstrap," an economic development program. The facility was built for a group of investors headed by Mr. Earl Crane of the Iroquois China Company, Syracuse, New York, in about 1947 – 1948. Earl Crane operated the facility until 1950, by which time he had exhausted the capital and the investment of the Puerto Rican government and shareholders. The shareholders began at this point to look for another stateside manufacturer to take over the operation.

It was at this point (fall of 1950) that the Sterling China Company of Wellsville, Ohio, became involved. Sterling took an option, later exercised that option, and began operating the facility in 1951. The plant had been designed as a hotel ware operation. In the late 1950s Caribe made a casual dinnerware line. They used their regular hotel ware body making for a superior product comparable only to Lenox's Casual ware line.

Caribe made about 12 patterns in their Casual dinnerware line, print transfer patterns, air brush, undecorated, and line decorated ware. Advertising information of the day credits Caribe dinnerware as being designed by Carlos Montez. Carlos Montez was a made-up name for Ed Murphy who was the initiator of the Caribe dinnerware idea.

The Caribe line was not competitive and was phased out in about 1962 – 1963. The plant was shut down in 1976 and liquidation neared completion.

The pieces that I have seen of Caribe are pleasing and of excellent quality, well worth a little extra search on the part of the collector.

Backstamps from Caribe dinnerware.

Caribe Casual plate, pattern unknown, $8.00 – 10.00. Cup/saucer set, $8.00 – 10.00. Mug, $6.00 – 8.00. The dinnerware is from the collection of Allen Kleinbeck. The hotel ware coffee mug is marked "Caribe."

Caribe ware advertisement for Bonita pattern.

Caribe ware advertisement for El Vuelo pattern.

Children's Dishes

Juvenile decorated mugs, plates, and other like pieces have long been a delight to search for and find. Whatever the reason for the attraction, from bunny-shaped plates to mugs, "Jack and Jill" juvenile ware has always appealed to the collector. The American pottery industry contributed its share of play dishes and feeding sets, with almost every major company producing such ware.

From the collection of John Moses and B. A. Wellman.

Row 1: Bunny plate, $45.00 – 50.00; Dick Tracy plate, $100.00 – 125.00; divided plate with chicken, $30.00 – 35.00.

Row 2: Three Little Bears plate, $20.00 – 25.00; matching Three Little Bears mug, $30.00 – 35.00; covered jug, $45.00 – 50.00; mug, $35.00 – 40.00; Froggie plate, $35.00 – 40.00.

Row 3: Mug, $35.00 – 40.00; mug, $35.00 – 40.00; same decal plate as previous mug, $30.00 – 35.00; mug, $35.00 – 40.00; mug, $30.00 – 35.00.

Page 45

Row 1: Part of a play set, teapot (no lid), $10.00 – 15.00; open sugar, $10.00 – 15.00; creamer, $15.00 – 20.00; cup/saucer, $15.00 – 20.00 set; Elmer mug, $45.00 – 55.00; Hankscraft bottle warmer, $15.00 – 20.00.

Row 2: Harker Cameo ware plate, $15.00 – 20.00; Cameo ware small plate, $15.00 – 25.00; Cameo ware mug, $15.00 – 18.00; Homer Laughlin "I go here says the fork" plate, made for International Silver, $25.00 – 30.00.

Row 3: Divided warmer feeding bowl, marked "Excello," Mexican scene, $40.00 – 45.00; divided feeding bowl, $25.00 – 30.00; divided warmer feeding bowl, Mary Had a Little Lamb, $25.00 – 30.00.

Row 4: All divided warmer feeding bowls. Harker bowl, $35.00 – 45.00; maker unknown, $25.00 – 30.00; maker unknown, $25.00 – 30.00; Hankscraft clown feeding dish, $40.00 – 45.00.

The Uncle Wiggily mug shown was "manufactured for The Wander Company, Chicago Makers of Ovaltine." The copyright date was 1924 and sole maker was the Sebring Pottery Company. $55.00 – 60.00.

Coors Pottery

Little is actually known about Coors. Pictured on page 47 is Coors' Rosebud line. Ms. Betty Latty, in a March 1977 article for *The Glaze*, suggests that Rosebud was probably introduced in the 1940s to compete with the popular Fiesta line by The Homer Laughlin Company. Ms. Latty also suggests that the Coors Mello-Tone line with its softer colors followed the Rosebud line.

Mello-Tone is not the best quality ware and the "rising sun" backstamp appears on Mello-Tone pottery. Coors Rosebud can be found in a wide variety of pieces and colors. Expect to pay slightly higher prices for Rosebud. Coors Mello-Tone pottery is found on their plain pastel line. Some of the Rosebud pieces are marked Coors, but most pieces are unmarked.

Page 47

Row 1: Cup, $12.00 – 15.00; custard cup, $15.00 – 20.00; handled soup bowl, $28.00 – 32.00; individual bowl, $15.00 – 20.00.

Row 2: Tab-handled bowl, $20.00 – 25.00; saucer, $6.00 – 8.00; 6" plate, $12.00 – 15.00; 8" plate, $15.00 – 18.00.

Row 3: Solid meat platter (no Rosebud decoration), $30.00 – 35.00; footed tumbler, $35.00 – 40.00; shaker, $15.00 – 18.00; 9" plate, $25.00 – 30.00; Coors advertising piece, $40.00 – 45.00.

Coors backstamp.

The Cronin China Company

The forerunner of the Cronin China Company in Minerva, Ohio, was the Owen China Company, built approximately in 1900. Dan Cronin moved his operation to Minerva and met an early death due to a riding accident. Surviving Cronin brothers managed the plant until it ceased operation in the fifties.

Mr. Dan Cronin and Mr. J. Block of Block China Company were friends. In the late thirties, Mr. Block founded the Pottery Guild, and Cronin China Company supplied at least some of the pieces of Pottery Guild ware. The corporation for Pottery Guild was granted in 1938 and cancelled in 1946 in the state of New York.

Pottery Guild pieces are pictured under Pottery Guild (see page 231). On rare occasions a piece may be found with both the Cronin and Pottery Guild backstamps.

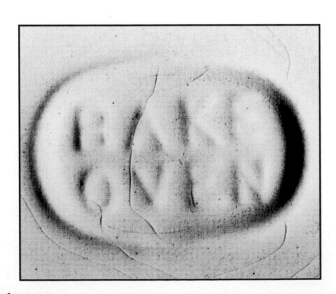

Cronin backstamps.

Crooksville China Co.

A group of Crooksville, Ohio, businessmen petitioned the Ohio Secretary of State for the purpose of granting a corporation for The Crooksville Art Pottery Company on January 9, 1902. S. H. Brown, W. H. Brown, W. J. Tague, A. P. Tague, and Guy E. Crooks were the petitioners. Crooksville Art Pottery was formed to manufacture art ware "such as vases, flower pots and novelties."

The first stockholders' meeting was held on January 20, 1902, and the following offices were elected:

President, J. L. Bennett; vice-president, J. M. French; secretary-treasurer and general manager Guy E. Crooks. After reviewing the activities in East Liverpool the board decided to amend the articles of their incorporation and the name was changed to Crooksville China Company.

A plant site was found and the W. H. Showers Construction Company broke ground for the plant in March 1902.

William Tritt of Sebring, Ohio, was hired as general superintendent and the first ware came out of the kiln in November of 1902. It was my pleasure to see one of those first pieces – a pitcher with one of the officer's name and date in gold. A personalized pitcher was made for each officer. By February 1903 the first ware was shipped by Pennsylvania Railroad. Mr. Tritt left Crooksville in 1910 when he moved to Niles, Ohio, to organize the Tritt China Company.

By 1923 more help was needed to oversee business, and Earl Crooks became assistant manager. S. L. Pitcock became assistant secretary and treasurer. Harry Bennett was elected to become president following his father's death in approximately 1941. The final closing was 1959.

The "Yel-o-Gren Cottage" outlet store for Crooksville China.

Crooksville China manufacturing plant.

The creamer and sugar with the Country Home scene are the only two pieces I have found. The Fruits blank was used with many different decals and I believe we can expect to find many more Country Home pieces. Creamer, $14.00 – 16.00; sugar and lid, $18.00 – 22.00.

Crooksville backstamp.

This delicate pattern was well remembered by Crooksville workers as they nicknamed it "Spider." Many companies used a decal so similar to this one that in some instances the collector has to rely on shapes and backstamps, not the decal, for identification. This Crooksville pattern was called other names by other stores and outlets. In this setting, everything but the creamer, sugar, and gravy are in the La Grande shape. The sugar, creamer, and gravy are in the Radisson shape. There are certainly many confusing factors in attempting to identify patterns and shapes of American dinnerware.

This pattern was listed in a 1940s wholesale catalog as "Spring Blossom."

Spring Blossom or "Spider" Haviland-like decoration. Top left: vegetable bowl, $15.00 – 18.00; Top right: large platter, $20.00 – 25.00; Middle left: sugar with lid, $18.00 – 20.00; creamer, $15.00 – 18.00; gravy boat, $15.00 – 18.00; oval vegetable bowl, $15.00 – 20.00; Lower left: fruit bowl $6.00 – 8.00; 10" plate, $12.00 – 14.00; 8" plate, $8.00 – 10.00; cup/saucer set, $12.00 – 15.00.

Crooksville backstamp.

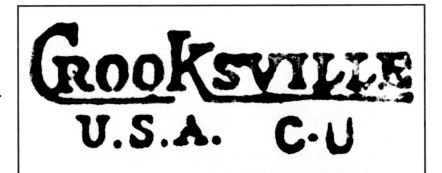

ESTABLISHED 1902

TRADE MARK
CROOKSVILLE
CHINA CO

THE CROOKSVILLE CHINA CO.

MAKERS OF

Dinner Ware

CROOKSVILLE, OHIO

NOTICE OF SHAREHOLDERS MEETING

Notice is hereby given that a meeting of the shareholders of The Crooksville China Company will be held at the office of the company on China Street, Crooksville, Ohio, on the 26th day of March, 1959, at 10:00 o'clock A.M., to consider and act upon the proposal for the final termination of the corporation, as set forth in the enclosed Memorandum.

By order of the Board of Directors.

Frank E. Bennett, Secretary

March 10, 1959

A letter from the Crooksville China Company to shareholders concerning final termination of the company, 1959.

Waffle sets were very popular in the 1920s and 1930s. This 1929 Crooksville waffle set consists of six 8" plates; one 11¼" serving or utility plate; one large covered jug for batter; one small covered jug for syrup; and six cup and saucer sets. The shapes of the jugs are referred to by collectors as "Duckbill." The jugs or pitchers set on the tray so, in some patterns, they are called batter sets.

Row 1: 8" Trellis plate, $10.00 – 14.00; Trellis utility tray, $30.00 – 35.00.

Row 2: Trellis covered batter pitcher, 8" tall including lid, $65.00 – 75.00; syrup pitcher, 6", with lid, $45.00 – 55.00; cup/saucer set, $15.00 – 18.00.

Crooksville backstamp.

Page 55 – All Silhouette.

Row 1: 8 oz. tumbler, $35.00 – 40.00; creamer, $25.00 – 30.00; utility bowl marked Pantry Bak-in, $45.00 – 50.00; utility bowl, also marked Pantry Bak-in, $35.00 – 40.00.

Row 2: 8" plate, $15.00 – 20.00; matching glass tumbler (not made by Crooksville), $25.00 – 30.00; pie baker, $30.00 – 35.00.

Row 3: 11¾" serving tray, $35.00 – 40.00; dinner plate, 10", $18.00 – 20.00.

Row 4: Platter, 11½", $30.00 – 35.00; lid, may fit a small spice jar, $10.00 – 15.00; saucer, $6.00 – 8.00.

$2⁹⁸
Sandwich and Bread Tray. Beautiful ivory colored china dish decorated with unique black silhouette figures. Handsome chromium plated frame in pierced and engraved design. Diameter 11¼ inches.
46 G 4337—We Pay Postage..........$2.98

$1³⁹ Candy or Relish Dish
Handsome pierced design chromium plated frame. Ivory colored China dish with black silhouette figures. Matches sandwich tray 46 G 4337. Diameter 6¾ inches. We Pay Postage.
46 G 4329 $1.39

1930 – 1931 Ward's catalog page showing sandwich and bread tray and candy dish in chrome plated frame. Crooksville's Silhouette differs from Hall's and is easily recognized by the begging dog whose mouth appears to be watering. This appealing pattern is available in a wide variety of interesting pieces including tankards, pitchers, kitchen covered utility jars, and covered refrigerator jars. Do not be surprised at any pieces you may find in Silhouette. The pattern is from the early 1930s and was also used with a Faberware frame backstamped Provincial Ware. The decal was used in the mid-1950s but the company that used the decal is unknown to me at this time.

Crooksville backstamp.

Row 1: Pheasant decoration on La Grande shape, 9" plate, $6.00 – 8.00; Mug, Hunting decoration, man with dog, $12.00 – 15.00; matching 12" plate with Hunting decoration, $15.00 – 20.00.

Row 2: Carnival decoration on what we previously called Fruits shape. The official name of this Crooksville shape is Euclid. 9½" plate, $12.00 – 14.00; Little Bouquet decoration on La Grande shape, 9¾" plate, $8.00 – 10.00; Homestead in Winter on Coupe shape Iva-Lure 10" chop plate, $10.00 – 15.00.

Page 57

Row 1: Southern Belle decoration, 6¾" plate on Coupe shape, $4.00 – 5.00; Avenue decoration saucer, pink Coupe shape, $4.00 – 5.00; Avenue covered sugar, $15.00 – 20.00; Apple Blossom decoration on La Grande shape saucer, $3.00 – 4.00; Apple Blossom 6" plate, $4.00 – 6.00.

Row 2: Apple Blossom decoration pie baker, marked Pantry Bak-In, $25.00 – 30.00; Apple Blossom two-handled bean pot, $55.00 – 65.00; Apple Blossom covered bowl, $35.00 – 40.00.

Row 3: Rose Garland bowl, 3" tall, $6.00 – 8.00; Rose Garland covered vegetable bowl, $20.00 – 25.00; Rose Garland gravy boat and liner, $12.00 – 15.00.

Row 4: Medallion saucer, $4.00 – 5.00; Border Rose covered vegetable bowl, $20.00 – 25.00; Border Rose platter, 11", $18.00 – 20.00.

Page 59

Row 1: Posies decoration on La Grande cup/saucer, $8.00 – 10.00 set; Posies decoration on small bowl, $6.00 – 8.00; Oriental decoration creamer, $10.00 – 14.00; Gold Drape decoration on creamer, $10.00 – 14.00.

Row 2: California James Poppy decoration on La Grande 10" plate, $10.00 – 12.00; California James Poppy decoration covered casserole, 8", marked Pantry Bak-in, $35.00 – 45.00; California James Poppy decoration platter, $20.00 – 25.00.

Row 3: Blue Blossoms decoration on two-handled bean pot, $55.00 – 65.00; Apple Blossom decoration on drip coffee maker base, $50.00 – 55.00.

Row 4: Blossoms decoration on 6¾" plate, $6.00 – 8.00; Roses decoration custard bowl, $6.00 – 8.00; Roses decoration on oblong bowl, $10.00 – 15.00; Kaleidoscope decoration on flat soup bowl, $8.00 – 10.00.

1930s catalog reprint showing how Pantry Bak-in ware was originally sold.

Black Tulip decoration, black on pink, designed by Arden Richards, circa 1950s. Plate, $20.00 – 25.00; divided vegetable dish, $25.00 – 30.00.

1980s correspondence with Crooksville workers told me this decoration was always called "House" or "Cottage." Since it is a Petit Point pattern I have called it "Petit Point House." The decoration was used on several different shapes as shown.

Page 61 – All Petit Point House decoration.
Row 1: Casserole (lid missing), $15.00 – 20.00. Complete with lid, $40.00 – 45.00; 7" plate, $8.00 – 10.00; server, $25.00 – 30.00.

Row 2: 9" plates, $10.00 – 12.00 each.

Row 3: Coupe shape serving plate, 12¾", $30.00 – 35.00.

Petit Point House teapot, $75.00 – 85.00.

Petit Point House cookie jar, $85.00 – 100.00.

Row 1: Avenue decoration on La Grande shape 10¾" dinner plate, $10.00 – 12.00; Avenue decoration on Coupe shape 10¾" dinner plate, $10.00 – 12.00; Calico Chick decoration on Coupe shape 10¾" plate, $10.00 – 12.00.

Row 2: Spray decoration on pink Coupe shape 10¾" dinner plate, $8.00 – 10.00; Flower Fair decoration on Coupe shape 9" plate, $10.00 – 12.00; Pink Border decoration on La Grande shape dinner plate, $10.00 – 12.00.

Row 3: Veggies 10" pie baker, marked Pantry Bak-in, $25.00 – 30.00; Rust Bouquet on La Grande shape 6" plate, $4.00 – 6.00; Rust Bouquet decoration on 10" pie baker, $25.00 – 30.00.

Page 63
Row 1: Hibiscus on Gray Lure (Gray Lure refers to the color of the glaze) 6" plate, $4.00 – 6.00; Hibiscus decoration creamer, $12.00 – 15.00; Hibiscus decoration sugar and cover, $15.00 – 18.00; Calico Flowers decoration on creamer, $12.00 – 15.00; sugar (lid missing), $8.00 – 10.00. Complete with lid, $20.00 – 25.00.

Row 2: Trotter decoration on 10¼" dinner plate, $8.00 – 10.00; cup and saucer set, $10.00 – 12.00; Scotch Plaid decoration on Coupe shape 10¼" dinner plate, $8.00 – 10.00.

Row 3: Trotter decoration on 7" Coupe shape plate, $6.00 – 8.00; Scotch Plaid decoration on 6" plate, $4.00 – 6.00.

Row 4: All four plates or saucers. Willow decoration on Coupe shape plate, $3.00 – 4.00; Blossom Time plate, $3.00 – 4.00; Rose Garden plate, $3.00 – 4.00; Jessie plate, $3.00 – 4.00.

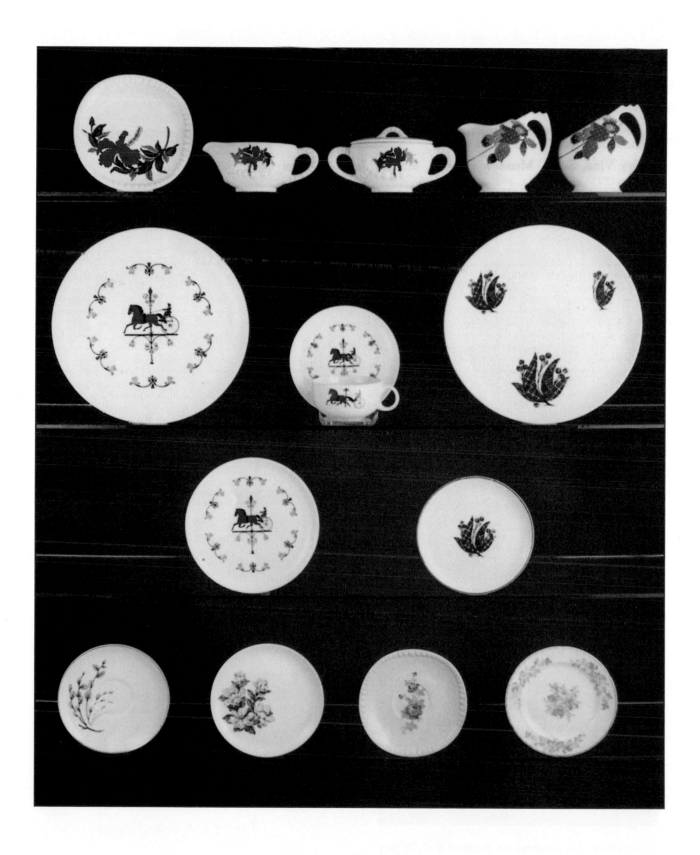

Page 65

Row 1: Southern Belle decoration on 7¾" plate, $6.00 – 8.00; Southern Belle covered sugar, $12.00 – 15.00; Southern Belle cup and saucer set, $12.00 – 15.00.

Row 2: Southern Belle decoration on 10¼" dinner plate, $8.00 – 10.00; Southern Belle decoration on 9" plate, $6.00 – 8.00.

Row 3: Brilliance decoration on Coupe shape 10¼" dinner plate, $8.00 – 10.00; Queen Rose decoration on 9" Coupe plate, $6.00 – 8.00; Border Bouquet decoration on La Grande shape 9" plate, $8.00 – 10.00.

Row 4: Ivy Vine decoration on Coupe shape, $8.00 – 10.00; Swirl decoration on 9" Coupe shape, $8.00 – 10.00; Meadow Flowers decoration on 9" Coupe shape, $8.00 – 10.00.

Oversize "Pop" cup/saucer, $10.00 – 12.00 set.

Modern Calla decoration plate, $10.00 – 12.00.

Rust Tulip decoration on Pantry Bak-in jug with lid, $35.00 – 45.00.

Pantry Bak-in backstamp.

Crown Potteries Co.

Crown Potteries Co. had its beginning as early as 1882 when it was established by A. M. Beck. In 1884 it was taken over by Bennighof and Uhl. The 1892 Evansville, Indiana, city directory mentions the incorporation of Crown Potteries in November of 1891 with H. V. Bennighof, president, Charles Uhl, secretary, and S. P. Gillatt, treasurer.

Other sources list the Flentke family as founding Crown in 1902 after an unsuccessful venture in Peoria, Illinois, but in our research we have been unable to connect the Flentke family as founders of Crown Potteries. John Wendt took over the management of Crown in the early days and retired in 1952. Management was taken over at that time by a Mr. Lundquest, who unsuccessfully attempted to halt the downward trend in business at Crown.

The pottery merged in the 1950s with Peerless Pottery, a maker of sanitary fixtures, and was finally closed in 1954.

A former Crown employee tells that to her knowledge there were no printed catalogs describing Crown. Sales were made by samples of ware carried by the salesmen. Crown made a semi-porcelain underglaze dinnerware with gold or platinum trims put on by hand. Patterns were not named but were known by numbers. New patterns came out each January and June.

Some of Crown's shape names were Jewel, Princess, Royal, Sovereign (see reprint), Majestic, Countess, and Regent — all in keeping with the name "Crown." The ovenware line consisted of pie bakers, bowls, syrup pitchers, and salt and pepper shakers.

The Princess shape was made mostly in plain white and fancy salad bowls, cake plates and servers, teapots, salad plates, and juvenile items.

Crown also came out with a line of colored dinnerware in green, blue, tangerine, and brown. Coronada is the name of Crown's colored ware line made to compete with the Fiesta ware that was popular in the 1940s.

Crown backstamp.

Crown's trademark.

1941 catalog reprint.

Page 69
Row 1: Croyden shape, Flower Border saucer, $2.00 – 3.00; gravy boat, $10.00 – 12.00; Spring Rose saucer, $2.00 – 3.00.

Row 2: Monarch shape 9" plate, $8.00 – 10.00; cup and saucer, $8.00 – 10.00 set; serving platter, $15.00 – 20.00.

Row 3: Monarch shape serving bowl, $12.00 – 15.00; cereal bowl, $4.00 – 6.00; 6" plate, $6.00 – 8.00.

Row 4: Autumn Leaf covered jug, $100.00 – 150.00; Carriage vegetable bowl, $15.00 – 18.00.

Colonial Dames casserole and cover, Princess decoration, $35.00 – 40.00.

Colonial Dames backstamp.

Rust Tulip decoration on embossed Tulip bowl, very unusual shape, $25.00 – 30.00.

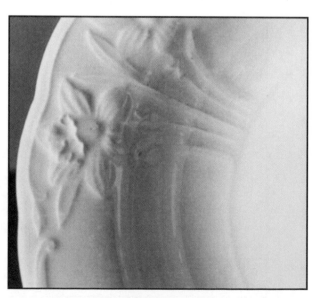

Close-up of embossing on Crown bowl.

Page 71

Row 1: All 6" plates. Flower Patch on Quena shape plate, $4.00 – 6.00; Rust Flowers on Sovereign shape plate, $4.00 – 6.00; Tiny Flowers on Monarch shape plate, $4.00 – 6.00; Deco Bouquet on Monarch plate.

Row 2: Princess decoration on Quena shape creamer, $12.00 – 14.00; Windmill decoration on kitchen/range shakers set, $20.00 – 25.00 set; Windmill decoration on pie baker, $25.00 – 30.00.

Row 3: Garden Gate decoration on 9" Monarch plate, $8.00 – 10.00; Poppy decoration on 9" plate, $8.00 – 10.00; Ribbon decoration ovenware pie baker, $20.00 – 25.00.

Row 4: Flower Garden decoration on 10" Quena shape plate, $8.00 – 10.00; Floral decoration on 9" ovenware pie baker, $20.00 – 25.00; Calico Flowers decoration on Sovereign shape 9" plate, $8.00 – 10.00.

Crown backstamps.

1941 Fort Dearborn catalog pate. Monarch and Quena shapes by Crown.

Cunningham & Pickett, Inc.

Cunningham & Pickett, Inc. was a sales organization that was founded about 1938 for the purpose of selling dinnerware and other items to grocery stores for their continuity programs. While they sold glassware, silverware, and other items, dinnerware was a major sales item, with about 90% of the dinnerware made by the Homer Laughlin China Company of Newell, West Virginia. Cunningham & Pickett's sales relationship with the Homer Laughlin Company began in 1938 and lasted until 1961.

Cunningham & Pickett, Inc. had several names they used over the years: the Alliance China Company, Lifetime China Company, Century Service Corportion, Kingsway China Company, International China Company, and International D. S. Company. By 1966 all of these companies were combined under the name of Cunningham Industries.

All of the ware purchased from the Homer Laughlin Company will have one of the Cunningham & Pickett names on the back of the pieces as well as the pattern name. These pieces are not commanding the same price and attention as the regular Homer Laughlin shapes and lines.

Cunningham & Pickett backstamps.

Frankoma

Frankoma was founded by John Frank. Frank came to Oklahoma from Chicago in 1927. In 1933 he started a studio pottery in Norman, Oklahoma, and equipped it with one small kiln, a butter churn for mixing clay, a fruit jar for grinding glazes, and a few other crude tools. He continued teaching until enough ware was produced to prove that a product could be made of Oklahoma clays that was a contribution to art and ceramics and still salable.

He resigned his teaching position in 1936 and he and Grace Lee, his wife, set out on their new venture. Oklahoma clays were used and by 1938 the studio was moved to Sapulpa, where it is still located.

Frankoma is manufactured by a once-fired process — clay body and colored glaze are fused and fired at the maturing point of the clay and tempered as it slowly cools.

Wagon Wheels is one of Frankoma's most popular lines.

Frankoma backstamp.

A reprint of a Frankoma ad.

French-Saxon China Company

During the early part of the Depression, W. V. Oliver liquidated his assets and put the money into several different banks, most of which had failed. His entire available assets amounted to $1,200 and faith in his abilities. It was at this point in his life he decided to buy Saxon, one of the Sebring potteries that was in the hands of the bank. Oliver took a thousand of the $1,200 to board members, and they accepted his offer. Now, Mr. Oliver had $200 left and needed to get the pottery operational. He went back to the banks where he had lost his money (some had reopened) and borrowed money.

The French-Saxon Company was opened. Vern Oliver was accustomed to "different beginnings." He had attended school only six months, and left home at the age of ten. His first job was delivering newspapers, then he went to work in a pottery. He became sales manager of Sebring Manufacturing Company, composed of the French China Company, the Saxon China Company, and Sebring Manufacturing Company. It was the Saxon plant that Oliver bought in 1934. With the help of Duncan Curtis, who handled French-Saxon's ware exclusively, the pottery was soon underway.

Vern Oliver passed away in 1963.

An article in the 1964 April issue of *China, Glass and Tableware* reports that Royal China purchased the French-Saxon Company of Sebring, Ohio. At that time (1964) Royalon, Inc. had manufacturing facilities in Sebring, East Palestine, Ohio, and Logansport, Indiana.

The French-Saxon shape shown is their Zephyr shape colored glaze dinnerware line popular in the mid-1930s. A wide assortment of decals was added on an ivory body in the late 1930s to the "already popular Zephyr shape" by French-Saxon. Poppy, Petit Point, and other decorations are found on the Zephyr shape. The pieces shown are from the collection of B.A. Wellman. Mr. Wellman tells us that, when French-Saxon added colors to this line, the name was changed to Rancho.

Backstamps from the French-Saxon China Company.

Page 77
Row 1: Rancho 10" dinner plate, $15.00 – 20.00; 9" plate, $8.00 – 10.00; dark green 6" plate, $4.00 – 8.00.

Row 2: Fruit bowl, $6.00 – 8.00; creamer, $15.00 – 20.00; "Go-with" glass tumbler made by Federal Glass Company, $18.00 – 20.00; cup and saucer, $13.00 – 16.00 set; cereal bowl, $8.00 – 12.00.

Row 3: Tangerine 9" plate, $15.00 – 18.00; cup and saucer, $13.00 – 16.00 set; creamer, $15.00 – 20.00; shaker, $9.00 – 10.00; sugar with cover, $20.00 – 25.00.

Catalog advertisement for Granada.

W. S. George Company

W. S. George was hired by the Sebring brothers to run the Ohio China Company in East Palestine, Ohio, in the mid-1890s. The Sebrings had been given $25,000 by the East Palestine townspeople plus free land to put up the Ohio building.

W. S. George managed to purchase the East Palestine Pottery Company in East Palestine by 1904. Soon after he is said to have suffered health problems. He later recovered and built a plant at Canonsburg and Kittanig, Pennsylvania, and a second plant in East Palestine that was known as the W. S. George #4 Plant.

Mr. George hoped to leave each one of his sons a pottery but only one son was interested in the pottery business. Some pieces will be marked Cavitt-Shaw Division of W. S. George. It is believed that Cavitt and Shaw were both family names. Cavitt-Shaw did not prove to be successful.

One of W. S. George's most popular patterns with collectors is Shortcake (see reprint on page 84) on the Ranchero shape.

Mr. Paul Merwin, retired newspaperman from East Palestine, has been very helpful with East Palestine's early history and shares the following early remembrances of W. S. George. We quote from a letter from Mr. Paul Merwin, dated December 19, 1979, and reprinted with written permission.

"Mr. George was a colorful personality, a boxer, a super salesman, and also a humanitarian. When business was slow, he would get on the train and sell. He always insisted his workers had a good Christmas pay — he would tell his foremen, make the ware, stockpile it if need be, I will sell it myself if necessary. At a meeting of officials of the United Presbyterian Church, held at Westminster College in New Wilmington, Pennsylvania, in the 1920s, the need for $125,000 was voiced by the missionary leaders to erect a hospital in Ethiopia. Mr. George rose to his feet and told the group, 'I'll take care of that item myself, let us proceed to the next order of business.' As a youngster, I recall him riding past our home in a silver-colored Pierce-Arrow, complete with chaffeur. He always sat in the back, behind a plate glass partition. He knew most of his employees by first name, would walk through the plants frequently, perhaps stopping at work benches to show an apprentice the 'right way to do things.'"

The W. S. George plant went out of business in the late 1950s. The Royal China operation used the W.S. George facility for a time for additional production.

W. S. George trademark.

Page 79
Row 1: All Lido shape. Blossoms. Covered sugar, $15.00 – 20.00; shaker, $8.00 – 10.00; creamer, $10.00 – 14.00; Dalyrymple decoration shakers, $18.00 – 22.00 set.

Row 2: All Lido shape. Blossoms 10" plate, $10.00 – 12.00; cup/saucer set, $10.00 – 12.00; flat soup, $10.00 – 12.00.

Row 3: Lido shape oval vegetable bowl, Mexican decoration, $25.00 – 30.00; saucer, $6.00 – 8.00; Lido shakers, Shortcake decoration, $15.00 – 18.00 set; Ranchero shape server, also Shortcake, $50.00 – 60.00.

Row 4: All Lido shape. Plain Jane 10" dinner plates, $10.00 – 12.00 each.

We now know that the "Petalware" shape's official name is Georgette and the decoration's name was officially Jolly Roger.

Elmhurst was introduced in 1939 in six pastel shades of blue, pink, yellow, Apple Green, Maple Sugar, and turquoise. Elmhurst shape had been previously introduced in 1937 but not in pastel glazes. In a 1937 trade publication, Elmhurst was described as having a "thinner body, delightfully modern and having a shape that harmonizes with new decal decorations."

W. S. George used the same shape shaker with several different shapes of patterns.

Row 1: All Georgette shape Jolly Roger decoration. Sugar (lid missing), $10.00 – 12.00; if complete with lid, $15.00 – 18.00; 9" plate, $10.00 – 12.00; creamer, $12.00 – 14.00.

Row 2: Saucer, $4.00 – 6.00; 7" plate, $6.00 – 8.00.

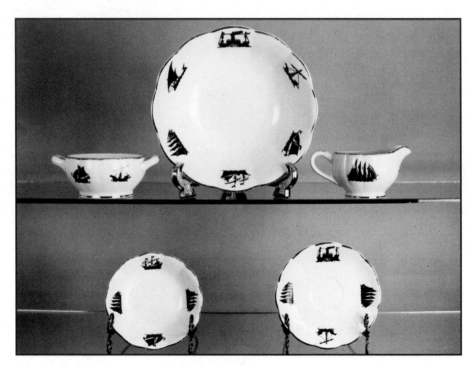

W. S. George backstamps.

Georgette and Rainbow Shapes

Row 1: All Georgette shape. Maroon plate, 9", $8.00 – 10.00; ivory fruit bowl, $6.00 – 8.00; dark green plate, $8.00 – 10.00.

Row 2: Pink 7½" plate, $8.00 – 10.00; pink sugar and cover, $20.00 – 25.00; light blue cup, $10.00 – 12.00; aqua saucer, $3.00 – 4.00.

Row 3: All Rainbow shape. Yellow saucer, $4.00 – 5.00; green cup, $12.00 – 15.00; blue egg cup, $25.00 – 30.00; green 5" bowl, $10.00 – 15.00; pink saucer, $8.00 – 10.00.

Page 83
Row 1: Both Lido shape 7" plates, $6.00 – 8.00 each.

Row 2: Rainbow shape Breakfast Nook 9" plate, $10.00 – 12.00; Rainbow Poppy decoration platter, $15.00 – 20.00; Fleurette shape Petit Point Rose 10" plate, $10.00 – 12.00.

Row 3: Rainbow 7" green plate, $10.00 – 12.00; blue fruit bowl, $6.00 – 8.00; yellow/tan 7" plate, $10.00 – 12.00.

Row 4: Derwood shape Bird plate, $18.00 – 20.00; 6" Bluebird plate, $15.00 – 20.00; Bolero shape fast-stand gravy boat, Roses decoration, $15.00 – 20.00; flat soup, $8.00 – 10.00.

Breakfast Nook on the Lido shape was introduced in late 1931 or early 1932. It was advertised in the trade papers as being "delicate and feminine," done in an antique "yelo-tinge" glaze.

By March of 1932, Breakfast Nook was being promoted by a large Chicago department store as "Spring-time" and a special sales promotion was used via direct mail and newspaper advertising. An entire window of the store on Chicago's State Street was devoted to a "Springtime" display.

This happened frequently in the matter of dinnerware names. Workers called a pattern one thing, the management another, and so on down the line. Each pattern shown in this book will have a name so that collectors will have a means of communication about this ware.

We did not have an example of Breakfast Nook on the Lido shape, but on the first plate in Row 2 on page 83, the Breakfast Nook decal is used on W. S. George's Rainbow shape.

W.S. George backstamp.

1940s magazine ad for W.S. George.

W.S. George backstamp.

Catalog reprint form Sears, Roebuck and Company showing Shortcake by W. S. George.

Row 1: Lido shape shaker designed by Simon Slobodkin (could go with other different floral decorations), $10.00 – 12.00; Ranchero shape Wampum decoration covered sugar bowl, $18.00 – 20.00; Wheat decoration coffee server, $35.00 – 40.00; Wampum creamer, $14.00 – 18.00; Lido shaker, Shortcake decoration, $10.00 – 12.00.

Row 2: All Lido shape (eggcups are probably an older shape). Flower Trim 10" plate, $8.00 – 10.00; Floral egg cup, $15.00 – 18.00; bowl, official decoration name Gaylea, $6.00 – 8.00; egg cup, Tiny Roses, $15.00 – 18.00; Cynthia 9" plate, $48.00 – 50.00.

Row 3: Rosita decoration on Ranchero shape gravy (marked Cavitt-Shaw), $14.00 – 16.00; Lido shape shaker, Blue Dawn decoration; Lido saucer, Pastel Floral, $4.00 – 6.00; ivory/gold-trim cream soup, $12.00 – 15.00; liner plate, $6.00 – 8.00; after-dinner Lido cup/saucer, $10.00 – 12.00 set; Lido shape Rust Floral cup, $4.00 – 6.00.

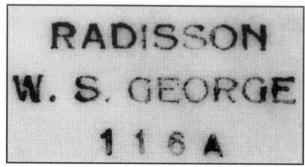

W. S. George backstamps.

W. S. George backstamp.

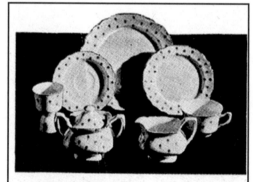

"BLUSHING ROSE"

28-Piece Service for Four

Tiny, red wild roses romp around each piece of this beautiful bright Breakfast and Luncheon service. Edged in gold and copied from an old Colonial print. Smooth inside and out. A perfect gift . . . especially for the newlyweds. A pattern and shape that will never grow old!

Set contains four each—salad and luncheon plates, cups and saucers, combination cereal and cream soups, egg cups, and of course, creamer, sugar and a large platter.

$9.50 Postpaid

THE COLONY SHOP
FORT WAYNE, INDIANA
Catalog on request

★ ★ ★ ★ ★ ★ ★ ★ ★ ★ ★ ★ ★ ★ ★

1940s magazine ad for W. S. George.

W. S. George backstamp.

Gonder

Again we are indebted to Mr. Norris Schneider for sharing his research by Lawton Gonder and the Gonder Ceramic Arts, Incorporated by way of an article written by Mr. Schneider that appeared in *Zane's Times Signal*, September 15 – 22, 1957.

Lawton Gonder quite literally grew up with potteries and pottery people. He went to work at the Ohio Pottery Company at the age of 13 running molds and casting handles. He went to work in 1915 for American Encaustic Tiling Company in the research department where he remained for 11 years. After a variety of different jobs, Gonder bought the former Zane Pottery Company and named it Gonder Ceramic Arts, Incorporated. Gonder manufactured a higher price art pottery. Two of his ideas that set him apart were flambe glazes described by Mr. Schneider as looking "like flame red with streaks of yellow." The other "innovation" was a gold crackle finish.

Not much dinnerware came out of the Gonder operation that we know of but what Gonder did manufacture is unique in styling, being very heavy and thick. La Gonda was made in the early 1950s.

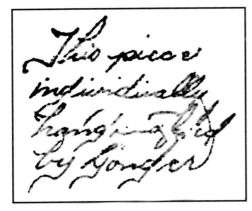   **Gonder backstamps.**

Row 1: La Gonda aqua cup, yellow saucer, $20.00 – 25.00 set; yellow covered sugar, $20.00 – 25.00; aqua 4½" bowl, $10.00 – 12.00.

Row 2: Pink sugar with cover, $20.00 – 25.00; aqua shaker, $15.00 – 18.00; pink 8½" luncheon plate, $18.00 – 20.00.

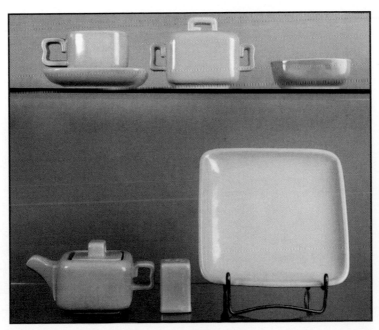

The Haeger Pottery

The Haeger Pottery was established in Dundee, Illinois, in 1871 as the Dundee Brick Yard. While Haeger is not primarily a dinnerware manufacturer, its earliest record of a dinnerware line dates back to 1919. Tableware and teaware were the two early lines. Haeger also had a children's tableware line with plate, cereal bowl, pitcher, mug, and plate. Tableware and teaware came in blue, rose, yellow, and green. In a 1927 catalog, the ware is shown in rich semi-matte black, Chinese blue, French blue, Meregreen, Ivory, and Mulberry.

A more recent and modern design in *Today's World* is Burnt Orange and Sandstone, made by the Haeger Pottery and designed by Ben Seibel. Another dinnerware line, Country Classics, is made in Stone Gray and Taupe, and was designed by the chief of Haeger's design division, C. Glenn Richardson.

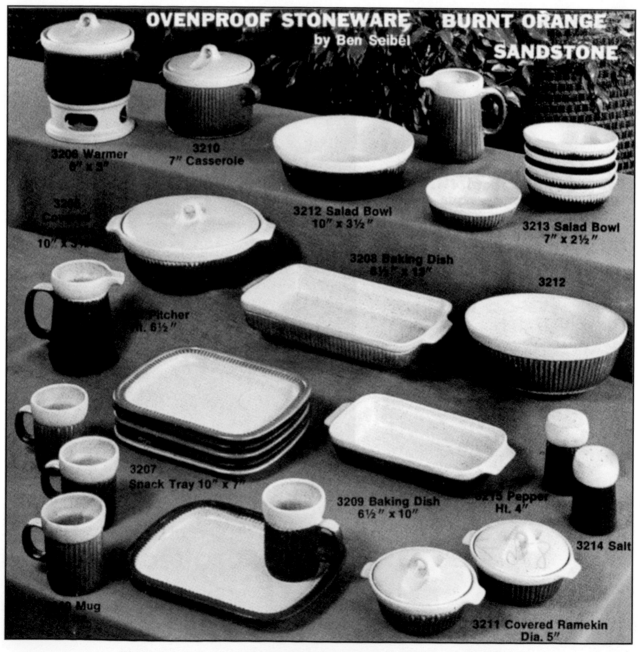

Photograph from a Haeger catalog, provided by the company.

Hall China Company

The Hall China Company was founded on August 14, 1903, in East Liverpool, Ohio, by Robert Hall. Thirty-three potters were employed and the first chinaware to bear the name of Hall were bedpans and combinets. The small company struggled for survival and whatever plans Mr. Hall had for its future were never known. Robert Hall died in 1904.

On Mr. Hall's death, his son, Robert Taggart Hall, became manager. He experimented tirelessly to develop a glaze that would withstand the heat required for bisque-firing. This single-fire process had been used during the Ming dynasty and this was all Mr. Hall had to go on, that it had been done before. Robert Taggart Hall developed the first leadless glaze in 1911. The pieces that came out of the kiln were strong, nonporous, and crazeproof. Temperatures used in the firing were 2400° F.

World War I gave The Hall China Company an opportunity to furnish ware to the institutional trade and they maintained this trade after the war. At this time, Hall became the world's largest manufacturer of decorated teapots and launched a campaign to educate the American housewife as to the proper methods of brewing tea. The proper pot was, of course, a Hall.

Continued success and obsolete equipment prompted the management to build a new factory in the east end of East Liverpool, Ohio. The plant was completed in 1930 and is still in operation at that site. Mr. John T. Hall is president and general manager. Hall also operates a plant in Gilmer, Texas, and has plans for building a plant at another site in Texas.

Row 1: Top left, Wild Rose covered casserole, $25.00 – 30.00; platter, $25.00 – 30.00.

Row 2: Center left, teapot, $175.00 – 185.00; covered Marmite bowl, $35.00 – 40.00; creamer, $18.00 – 20.00.

Row 3: Cereal bowl, $8.00 – 10.00; 7" plate, $6.00 – 8.00; flat soup, $15.00 – 18.00, 9" plate, $10.00 – 12.00; cup, $12.00 – 14.00.

Page 91

Row 1: Stonewall or Basket covered casserole, $45.00 – 50.00. It is one of three stackette refrigerator sets #296. There was only a small amount of this decal used. You will find other items with this decal, salt & pepper and others, made from 1932 to 1960, but not a big market; decoration #488 creamer, $18.00 – 20.00. Made in six sizes with or without covers. Numbers 282, 283, 284, 285, 286, and 287 made for general retail trade, dating back to 1930; a good seller; Fantasy decoration on ball jug, $175.00 – 185.00. It can be found in several pieces and dates back to the late 1930s and early 1940s. These jugs were made in these numbers, smallest #1631, #1632, #1633, and largest, #1634.

Row 2: Clover decoration #286 jug, $75.00 – 80.00. Several items with this decal were made for retail trade, probably 1940 – 1960. Blue Blossom on cobalt blue ball jug, $125.00 – 150.00.

Row 3: Eva Zeisel Bouquet Hallcraft jug, $35.00 – 40.00; pie baker made for Forman Brothers, $30.00 – 35.00.

Row 4: Canary yellow baking dish in metal frame made for Manning Bowman Company, mid-1930s, #1831 tea jar, part of canister set, made in many colors and decorations, $65.00 – 75.00.

Hall backstamps.

Page 93
Row 1: Three sizes of china jugs designed by Joseph Palin Thorley. #1540, $30.00 – 35.00; #1538, $25.00 – 30.00; #1536, $15.00 – 20.00.

Row 2: Monticello decoration for E-shape dinnerware for Sears, also designed by Joseph Palin Thorley. 10" plate, $10.00 – 12.00; platter, $20.00 – 25.00.

Row 3: Monticello cup and saucer, $13.00 – 16.00 set; covered sugar, $20.00 – 22.00; covered casserole, $35.00 – 40.00.

Row 4: Mt. Vernon two-piece all-china dripper coffee maker made exclusively for Sears, $45.00 – 50.00.

    J. Palin Thorley was a designer for Hall China in the 1940s. The Thorley jugs were made only in white with gold trim. If you look closely at the Sears E-shape dinnerware reprint below, you will see Duncan Phyfe styled candleholders designed by Mr. Thorley for Hall.

Hall Monticello backstamp.

Sears catalog reprint.

Cameo Rose – E-Shape

Cameo Rose was made exclusively for the Jewel Tea Company by The Hall China Company, East Liverpool, Ohio. It was available in the Jewel Home Shopping Service catalogs in open stock into the early seventies. It is a very popular pattern with collectors. A word of caution: the cup handles tend to "pop-off"; check for glued or mended handles.

Save up to 19% on Cameo Rose

(D) "Cameo Rose." Now available at reduced prices! We will be discontinuing this pattern soon, so take advantage of this opportunity to purchase lovely "Cameo Rose" ware at special prices. Superior quality semi-vitreous ware has a hard-fired, non-porous glaze...will not fade or craze. Decorative rose bud and leaf border with gold line trim frames the single White rose.

16-Piece Breakfast Starter Set includes: 4 cups, 4 saucers, 4 fruit dishes and 4 breakfast plates.
*5R 1. Was 10.95....Now 8.88

16-Pc. Dinner Starter Set includes: 4 cups, 4 saucers, 4 fruit dishes and 4 dinner plates.
*5R 52. Was 11.95...Now 9.88

53-Piece Service for 8. (See composition of set listed at right above.)
*5R 53. Was 42.95. Now 35.88

53-Pc. Set consists of 8 cups, 8 saucers, 8 fruit dishes, 8 bread & butter, 8 salad and 8 dinner plates plus large platter, oval vegetable dish, covered sugar bowl and creamer.

Open Stock	Cat. No.	Was	Now
Cup	*5R 2	.90	.76
Saucer, 6"	*5R 4	.50	.42
Bread & Butter, 6½" .	*5R 6	.60	.51
Salad Plate, 6½"	*5R 7	.80	.68
Pie Plate, 8"	*5R 8	.95	.81
Breakfast Plate, 9¼" .	*5R 9	1.10	.93
Dinner Plate, 10" . . .	*5R 10	1.45	1.23
Small Platter, 11½" . .	*5R 11	1.90	1.61
Large Platter, 13¼". .	*5R 13	3.10	2.63
Fruit Dish, 5¼" . .	*5R 15	.55	.47
Cereal Dish, 6¼" . .	*5R 16	.95	.81
Soup-Coupe, 8"	*5R 17	1.10	.93
Sugar Bowl Complete .	*5R 18	3.90	3.31
Creamer.	*5R 21	2.00	1.70
Oval Veg. Dish, 10½"	*5R 25	2.85	2.42
Cov. Veg. Dish.	*5R 26	7.50	6.37
Gravy Boat.	*5R 29	3.10	2.63
Pickle Dish, 9"	*5R 30	1.50	1.27
Round Veg. Dish, 8¾"	*5R 32	2.85	2.42
Salt Shaker.	*5R 38	1.10	.93
Pepper Shaker.	*5R 39	1.10	.93
Cream Soup	*5R 40	2.25	1.91
Tid-Bit Tray.	*5R 42	4.75	4.04
Cov. Butter Dish, ¼lb	*5R 43	2.25	1.91
Cov. Tea Pot, 6-cup. .	*5R 51	5.50	4.67

Catalog reprint showing Cameo Rose by Hall China Company and the original prices.

Hall's Cameo Rose backstamp.

Row 1: Cameo Rose cup and saucer set, $12.00 – 15.00; fruit dish, $4.00 – 6.00; creamer, $12.00 – 14.00; covered sugar, $14.00 – 18.00.

Row 2: Cameo Rose covered vegetable dish, $50.00 – 60.00; salt and pepper set, $35.00 – 40.00; teapot, $75.00 – 80.00.

Row 3: Cameo Rose 10" dinner plate, 3-tier tidbit server, $60.00 – 65.00; 7¾" plate, $6.00 – 8.00.

Row 1: Fuji creamer, $15.00 – 20.00; covered sugar, $20.00 – 25.00; coffee maker, $125.00 – 135.00; server coffee server, $65.00 – 75.00.

Row 2: Fuji Petite Marmites (pronounced Marmeat) in chrome frame. Foods can be kept warm or cold. Set complete with Manning-Bowman frame, $150.00 – 160.00.

Page 97
Row 1: Open sugar, Rose Parade, Sani-Grid shape, #2293, $18.00 – 20.00; Cadet blue Rose Parade #2286, salt and #2287 pepper, white handles, $15.00 – 18.00 each; #633 Cadet blue ball jug, $50.00 – 60.00.

Row 2: Wildfire decoration #1186 salt, pear shape, $18.00 – 20.00; #988 covered drip jar, $20.00 – 25.00; pear shape pepper shaker, #1187, $18.00 – 20.00.

Row 3: Wildfire mixing/utility bowl, #2277, $25.00 – 30.00; #3075 coffee server/drip bottom, $55.00 – 60.00. The #3075 was a special item for The Great American Tea Company. The lid has an "S" on it.

Row 4: Pastel Morning Glory salt shaker, pear shape, #1186, $18.00 – 20.00; Mums decoration (used from 1932 – 1969) large mixing bowl, $25.00 – 30.00; smaller bowl, $12.00 – 16.00; Heather Rose salad bowl, #3078, $15.00 – 20.00.

Orange Poppy

Decal #414 made for The American Tea Company.

Row 1: Range handled salt, #1186, $15.00 – 20.00; handled pepper, #1187, $15.00 – 20.00; #361 custard, $6.00 – 8.00; mustard jar (lid missing) if complete, $120.00 – 125.00.

Row 2: Ball jug, #633, $35.00 – 40.00; #3116 Do-nut teapot, $400.00 – $420.00; #286 open jug, $35.00 – 45.00.

Row 3: 8" round casserole, #78, $30.00 – 35.00; 7¼" plate, $10.00 – 12.00; non-Hall round jar, lid missing. If complete, $55.00 – 65.00; as is, $35.00 – 40.00.

Expect to find many other pieces in Orange Poppy, both in Hall China and accessory items. There is an Orange Poppy tablecloth and step-on metal trash can.

Autumn Leaf

Autumn Leaf is the most popular dinnerware pattern ever produced at the Hall plant. Autumn Leaf was made by Hall for the Jewel Tea Company from 1933 until 1976. Not all pieces were made continuously during that time.

This is but a sampling of the many different pieces made in this pattern. In many of the dinnerware patterns one is able to find matching glassware and tinware. In the case of the popular Autumn Leaf, plastic items and linens are also sought after by collectors.

Autumn Leaf was an exclusive line made only for Jewel and sold only through Jewel Companies. The decal, however, was not exclusive and was found on pieces made by just about every major manufacturer of dinnerware in the early 1930s. The decal became exclusive at some later point.

Two-cup teapot (Boston shape) used in the corporate offices of the Jewel Home Shopping Service. Only six or eight known and not ever nationally distributed. No price established.

Hall China backstamps.

Page 101

Row 1: Autumn Leaf three-piece mustard jar or condiment jar, $85.00 – 95.00; cream soup, $30.00 – 35.00; teacup, $12.00 – 14.00; St. Denis cup, $25.00 – 28.00.

Row 2: Autumn Leaf gravy boat, $30.00 – 35.00; teapot (also promoted as a four-cup dripolator), $85.00 – 90.00; one-pound butter dish, $400.00 – 475.00.

Row 3: Autumn Leaf St. Denis saucer, $8.00 – 10.00; metal flour sifter (not made by Hall), $450.00 – 525.00; saucer, $3.00 – 4.00.

Row 4: Autumn Leaf 10" dinner plate, $12.00 – 14.00; bud vase, $175.00 – 195.00; Libbey Glass frosted tumbler, $18.00 – 26.00; ball jug, $40.00 – 45.00.

All Hall China Autumn Leaf pieces will have the Mary Dunbar name included in the backstamp. The fluted vase shown is the only one found to date. It is believed to be a sample item only. No price established.

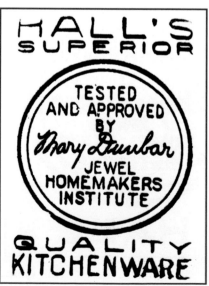

Hall China backstamps.

Page 103

Row 1: Serenade decoration on 8" plate, teacup, $8.00 – 10.00; creamer, $14.00 – 16.00; 4" fruit/sauce dish, $4.00 – 6.00.

Row 2: Serenade 9" plate, $10.00 – 12.00; New York six-cup teapot, $140.00 – 145.00; coffee pot (metal drip missing), $50.00 – 60.00.

Row 3: Poppy covered kitchen jars, made for the R.H. Macy Company in the 1930s. The set consists of a sugar, tea, coffee, and flour jar, salt and pepper shakers, and several other pieces.

Row 4: All Acacia, may be found in several different colors and decorations, shapes date back to the 1930s. Pear shape #1186 salt, $20.00 – 25.00; covered drippings jar #488, $25.00 – 35.00; covered casserole #298, $45.00 – 55.00; Marmite #474, $50.00 – 60.00.

Hall China backstamp.

Hall China: All Crocus decal #6130 platinum lines, made since about 1938 and sold to retail trade and some tea compnnies. The decals were cut in pieces to get the maximum use. The cut pieces are called Srig and the complete decal was called a border decal. Some stores and gas stations used Crocus as premium.

Crocus St. Denis cup is just one of the more recent finds in the Crocus pattern. The Crocus St. Denis cup is from the collection of Don and Irma Brewer. The Brewer's also have a beautiful soup tureen in the Crocus pattern. $45.00 – 55.00 set.

Page 105
Row 1: Crocus decoration decal #6130 creamer, $30.00 – 35.00; covered sugar, $45.00 – 50.00; beverage mug, $50.00 – 60.00; D-Shape creamer, $20.00 – 25.00; D-Shape covered sugar, $30.00 – 35.00.

Row 2: Crocus decoration D-Shape gravy, $35.00 – 45.00; Radiance drip jar and cover, $30.00 – 35.00; handled salt and pepper, $18.00 – 22.00 each.

Row 3: Crocus decoration #633 ball jug, $150.00 – 175.00; New York teapot border decal, $180.00 – 190.00; coffeepot, $150.00 – 200.00.

Row 4: Crocus #278 decoration mixing bowl, (part of set), $35.00 – 40.00; pretzel jar bean pot, $190.00 – 210.00; #298 casserole and cover, $50.00 – 55.00.

All Crocus Decal #6138, Sprig Layout, D-Shape
Platinum Lines

Page 107

Row 1: All Crocus decoration. Cup, $14.00 – 16.00; saucer, $2.00 – 3.00; cereal bowl, $8.00 – 10.00.

Row 2: Round vegetable bowl, 9", $20.00 – 25.00; oval vegetable bowl, $20.00 – 25.00; flat soup, $25.00 – 30.00.

Row 3: 9" plate, $18.00 – 20.00; 8" plate, $8.00 – 10.00; 7" plate, $8.00 – 10.00.

Row 4: 12" platter, $30.00 – 35.00; 10" platter, $25.00 – 30.00.

Original Hall China Crocus advertising photograph, late 1930s.

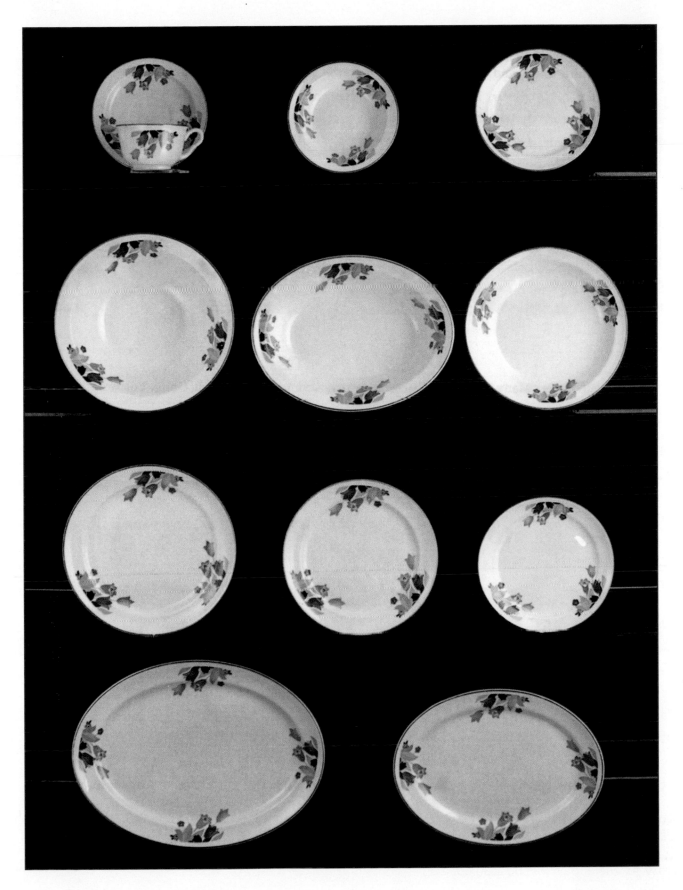

Silhouette

Silhouette was a premium item of The Cook Coffee Company and also of The Standard Coffee Company in the 1930s and 1940s. Do not be surprised at any piece you may find with Silhouette decal. Both Hall China and Taylor, Smith & Taylor used this pattern. The Harker Company made the rolling pins.

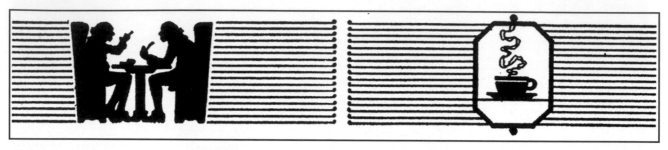

Silhouette shelf paper. Many accessory pieces were designed to go with Hall China but were not made by Hall.

Reproduction of actual salesmen's route cards for Cook Coffee Company, Detroit, Michigan, dated 7/31/42.

Page 109

Row 1: Silhouette shelf paper, each package, $50.00 – 60.00; Harker rolling pin, $125.00 – 130.00; MacBeth-Evans glass pitcher, $100.00 – 150.00.

Row 2: Silhouette metal wax paper dispenser, $50.00 – 55.00; metal shakers, $12.00 – 15.00 each.

Row 3: Metal match safe, $40.00 – 45.00; kitchen utensils (worn with some of the decoration off), $10.00 – 12.00 each; if mint $20.00 – 25.00 each; metal sitter, $45.00 – 50.00.

Row 4: Metal tray, $25.00 – 30.00.

Westinghouse Electrical Appliances

List Prices Subject to Catalog Discount—See Page 1A

Limited Supply   **W**   Limited Supply

WESTINGHOUSE
FOOD CRAFTER
Illustrated at Left

EE4165 .... **$37.50**
(Suggested Retail Price $46.95)

Food Crafter with beaters and two Hall Fireproof China bowls; permanently attached rubber armored cord with soft-rubber unbreakable attachment plug; for AC or DC operation.

- Built-in power unit.
- No extra gear needed for attachments.
- Beaters are easily inserted, locking into place automatically.
- Beaters drop out at the touch of button but will not fall into bowl.
- Food Crafter Motor—non-radio interfering.
- Approved by Underwriters Laboratory.

From a 1940s wholesale catalog. Hall made several items for Westinghouse during these years. Refrigerator sets and baking pans for roasters were just some of the items made for Westinghouse during this period.

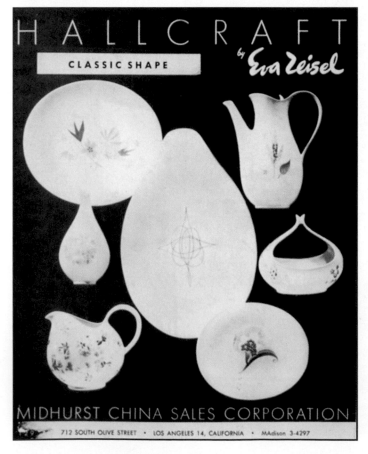

HALLCRAFT
CLASSIC SHAPE
by Eva Zeisel

MIDHURST CHINA SALES CORPORATION
712 SOUTH OLIVE STREET • LOS ANGELES 14, CALIFORNIA • MAdison 3-4297

HALLCRAFT
BY
Eva Zeisel

MADE IN U. S. A. BY HALL CHINA CO.

Hallcraft was a line designed for Hall China Company by Eva Zeisel. The Classic Shape came in a myriad of patterns plus Hallcraft white. Some holloware pieces were available in Satin Black or Satin Grey. The holloware pieces available in Black Satin finish were: salt and pepper, after-dinner cream and sugar, six-cup coffeepot, six-cup teapot, gravy boat, 12 oz. sugar, and 13 oz. creamer, after-dinner cup, teacup. Available also in grey finish were: salt and pepper, after-dinner 6 oz. sugar, six-cup coffeepot, six-cup teapot, gravy boat, 12 oz. sugar, 13 oz. creamer, after-dinner saucer, and tea saucer.

I. W. Harper Decanter

Not dinnerware, but a striking example of other items made by the American pottery industry. Hall China made several different figural bottles over a period of about 25 years.

I.W. Harper decanter, $100.00 – 125.00.

Flare Ware Gold Lace made by the Hall China Company in the 1960s. Other known pieces are #1765 coffee server with brass warmer teapot, coffee urn, three-pint casserole, cookie jar, three-piece bowl set, and salad bowl.

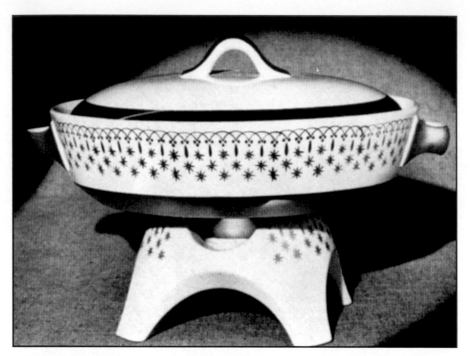

Reprinted from *China, Glass & Tableware*, Clifton, New Jersey.

Guaranteed against cracking under ordinary oven conditions is this colorful plaid china, for kitchen or buffet service, including two covered dishes and mixing bowls which might double for fruit or salad. (Hall China Company)

1932 ad for Hall China.

1927 Hall Cattail coffee server.

The Harker Pottery Co.

The Harker Company had its beginning in 1840 when Benjamin Harker, an English slater (roofer) came to America and bought a farm for $3,600 on the banks of the Ohio River at East Liverpool, Ohio. The farm had extensive clay deposits and for a year or so, Harker sold clays to James Bennett who later founded the Bennett Pottery Company. It occurred to Harker that he might make pots and he ceased to sell to Bennett. In 1840, he and his sons, George and Benjamin, Jr., built a kiln and soon were transporting yellow ware dishes by boats and wagons.

Soon after the new business was underway, Benjamin Harker died and his sons took over the operation. All was well until the Civil War. One brother was drafted and the other brother died, leaving the small pottery without a manager. At this time, a brother-in-law, David Boyce, took over the operation for the remaining Harker brother. David Boyce was married to Jane Harker, sister of the Harker boys.

After the war, the remaining Harker boy returned to the pottery but the name of Boyce was to remain an important name to the Harker operation from that time on.

Harker began making whiteware in 1879. There was quite a celebration of Harker employees and employers when the first kiln of whiteware was drawn. Harkers and their employees ferried to Rock Springs where they celebrated by consuming ten kegs of beer and dancing to the music of the East Liverpool brass band.

The pottery was put into very bad financial straits by a severe flood in 1884. Workers were paid by check and had to hold those checks until the bank balance covered them, but the Harker Company boasts that none of their workers missed a pay period. Charles R. Boyce is given credit for the growth and success of The Harker Company. Robert E. Boyce, oldest son of Charles, joined the company in 1923 and became the factory's ceramic engineer in 1927. David G. Boyce, another son, began selling dinnerware in the summer of 1923 and later served as president of The Harker Company.

By 1931, the company was relocated to Chester, West Virginia, across the river from the East Liverpool site. It was felt that the threat of floods was too great at the old site. In 1965, the Harker organization is said to have employed 300 people and was capable at full production of turning out some 25 million pieces of dinnerware annually. In 1945 the company also introduced its exclusive process using a copper engraving device. The decorations themselves are in white and were carved from engobe colors. Engobe is "white or colored slip applied to earthenware after as a support for a glaze or enamel." Collectors refer to this Harkerware as "Cameoware." It was made in a variety of base colors with White Rose in blue being most common.

The Jeannette Glass Company bought Harker and closed it down in March of 1972. Another company, Ohio Stoneware, Inc., made crockpot liners in the building until it was totally destroyed by a fire in September of 1975.

"The oldest pottery in America" is used on some Harker backstamps. While Harker was one of the oldest continuously run dinnerware plants and certainly one of the oldest in the East Liverpool, Ohio, area, it can hardly lay claim to being the oldest pottery in America.

The corporate name for the Harker operation was Harker Pottery. The name of Harker China was used in the 1950s to identify and probably to promote their chinaware line.

Harker backstamps.

Mallow

One of Harker's most attractive decorations is Mallow. The Mallow baking set complete with original wire rack and metal lids is valued at $45.00 – 60.00 for the complete set.

Rose Spray

Rose Spray is an all-over decoration of tiny pink flowers tinged with yellow trimmed in a flat gray. The Rose Spray set boasts a wide variety of serving pieces.

Top row, left to right: 9" breakfast plate, $12.00 – 15.00; 6" round plate, $10.00 – 15.00; 8" serving bowl, $10.00 – 15.00; tab-handled-bowl, $10.00 – 15.00; two-handled soup bowl, $15.00 – 20.00; cup, $10.00 – 15.00.

Front row, left to right: Creamer, $15.00 – 25.00; 10" dinner plate, $13.00 – 15.00; square luncheon plate, $15.00 – 18.00; cup/saucer set, $15.00 – 25.00.

Page 117
Row 1: Regal pitcher, Blue Blossoms decoration, $20.00 – 25.00; Rosebud shaker, $6.00 – 8.00; small pitcher, $30.00 – 40.00.

Row 2: Regal pitcher, Boyce decoration, gold trim handle, $20.00 – 25.00; saucer with Cherry Trim decoration, $5.00 – 7.00; saucer with Basket decoration, $4.00 – 6.00.

Row 3: English Countryside decoration on tall jar, lid missing, $25.00 – 35.00; individual custards or bake dishes, $10.00 – 15.00 each.

Row 4: Jessica decoration on large utility/mixing bowl, $30.00 – 45.00; Brim decoration on 9" snack plate, $10.00 – 12.00.

Harker HotOven backstamps.

Page 119

Row 1: Salt and pepper set, not made by Harker, may be Cronin, $12.00 – 15.00 set; server, $10.00 – 15.00.

Row 2: 7" Regal pitcher with Fruits decoration, $50.00 – 75.00; platter with Cherry Blossom decoration, $12.00 – 15.00.

Row 3: Modern Tulip platter, $8.00 – 15.00; lifter, $8.00 – 15.00; server, $8.00 – 10.00; rolling pin, $25.00 – 50.00. The Modern Tulip decoration is not in great demand at this time so prices are lower than anticipated.

Row 4: Autumn Leaf decorations on items are very desirable to collectors. Autumn Leaf decoration on 9" Harker plate, $50.00 – 75.00; individual custard or baking dish, $20.00 – 25.00; 10" utility/mixing bowl, $80.00 – 90.00; 9" utility/mixing bowl (not shown), $70.00 – 85.00.

Columbia Chinaware

Columbia Chinaware was a sales organization owned by the Harker Pottery Co. and operated by Harker. The Columbia Chinaware was in business from approximately 1935 to 1955. Not only did the company have Harker dinnerware and baking ware but other items including enamel ware, glass, and aluminum items. The sales organization generally went into smaller towns and not the larger cities. Mr. Boyce told me that letters from customers had stated they preferred Columbia products over Harker, an amusing bit of trivia in view of the fact that Columbia and Harker were one and the same. There is a remote possibility that wares sold by Columbia other than dinnerware were marked Columbia in some way. At this point, that is conjecture and not based on fact. Columbia Chinaware was a sales subsidiary of the Harker Pottery Company.

Harker Columbia backstamp.

Page 121

Row 1: All Amy decoration. Sugar (lid missing), $15.00 – 18.00; creamer, $15.00 – 18.00; server, $15.00 – 18.00; individual casserole, $8.00 – 15.00; individual baker, $8.00 – 15.00.

Row 2: Amy decoration 9" plate, $8.00 – 10.00; 7" plate, $7.00 – 9.00; 6" plate, $6.00 – 8.00; saucer, $4.00 – 6.00.

Row 3: Amy teapot, $35.00 – 50.00; hard-to-find scoop, $50.00 – 75.00; fork, $15.00 – 18.00; spoon, $15.00 – 18.00; platter, $15.00 – 25.00; rolling pin, $50.00 – 75.00.

Row 4: Amy decoration on High-Rise jug with lid, $75.00 – 85.00; tab handle soup, $10.00 – 12.00; utility bowl, $25.00 – 35.00; four-piece stack set with lid, complete, $25.00 – 35.00.

Harker Bakerite backstamp.

Mallow and Pansy

Page 123
Row 1: Pansy decoration on 6" bowl, $5.00 – 7.00; Pansy pepper shaker, $8.00 – 10.00; Mallow lard jar, $15.00 – 25.00; Mallow small covered jug, $30.00 – 40.00.

Row 2: Mallow decoration on 8" plate, $7.00 – 10.00; serving spoon, $15.00 – 20.00; 7½" bowl, $15.00 – 17.00.

Row 3: Mallow 10"utility/mixing bowl, $25.00 – 35.00.

Row 4: Mallow 12" utility/serving plate, $20.00 – 25.00; Mallow decoration on utility/serving plate, more ornate treatment, $18.00 – 25.00.

All Mallow. Small bowl, Sprig treatment, $12.00 – 15.00; flat bowl, $30.00 – 35.00; custard, $15.00 – 18.00.

Page 125

Row 1: Lisa server, $15.00 – 18.00; Lisa spoon, $15.00 – 18.00.

Row 2: Lisa utility/mixing bowl, $35.00 – 40.00; 7" plate, $7.00 – 10.00.

Row 3: Ruffled Tulip covered bowl, complete with lid, $20.00 – 25.00; Ruffled Tulip utility/serving tray 11¾", $15.00 – 20.00; Ruffled Tulip on Arches jug, complete with lid, $30.00 – 45.00.

Row 4: Lisa on Arches utility/mixing bowl, $25.00 – 35.00; Becky utility bowl, $25.00 – 30.00; Florist bowl with Poppy decoration, $25.00 – 55.00.

Harker Royal Gadroon backstamp. (See page 128).

Harker Hot Oven Line
Petit Point Rose

Just about every American manufacturer of dinnerware used a Petit Point type of decal on one or more of its lines. The most popular type of Petit Point seemed to be roses or flowers. Other designs were used, however, and it will be interesting to see just what was made in Petit Point.

Notice, please, the variations in the decals shown. I will refer to the more ornate and detailed decal as Petit Point Rose I and the other will be called Petit Point Rose II. There will be pieces that will seemingly not fit into either category and I will refer to those pieces as Petit Point Rose.

Petit Point Rose and Rose I & II

Page 127

Row 1: Rose II cake server, $12.00 – 15.00; Rose II individual custard, $8.00 – 10.00; Rose I individual baker, $8.00 – 12.00; Rose I server, $12.00 – 15.00.

Row 2: Rose II utility/mixing bowl, 11½" across top, $30.00 – 35.00; Rose II covered casserole, $25.00 – 35.00.

Row 3: 9" pie baker, Rose I, $15.00 – 20.00; rolling pin, $50.00 – 90.00; 6" plate, $6.00 – 8.00; Rose II pie baker, $15.00 – 20.00; matching rolling pin, $50.00 – 75.00.

Row 4: Rose II small utility bowl, 3¾" deep, 6" across top; middle bowl, 3½" deep, 6½" across top; large bowl, 4¾ deep, 7½" across top. $85.00 – 110.00 set.

Harker's Royal Gadroon shape was achieved by spraying slip on the surface and wiping the Gadroon edge. The Chesterton line was actually the Royal Gadroon shape offered in gray, green, yellow, pink, and blue. It was not popular in the pink and blue colors.

Paté sur paté was achieved by spraying engobe with a mask or using a mask after drying to blast the design. This method cut through the engobe, eliminating decals.

Puritan was another name given to the Royal Gadroon shape to distinguish it from decorated Royal Gadroon. Puritan was plain white and attractive without decals.

Mr. Boyce says that Royal Gadroon ashtrays were sold by the thousands from 1945 – 1965. They sold to hotels, etc., for 15¢ each and up, depending on quantity. (See advertising pieces on page 15)

All Royal Gadroon shape, assorted decals.

Row 1: Small 6" plate; saucer; 6" plate; 6" plate; $4.00 – 6.00 each.

Row 2: 8" plates. $5.00 – 7.00; $8.00 – 10.00; $8.00 – 12.00.

Row 3: 8" plates. $5.00 – 8.00 each.

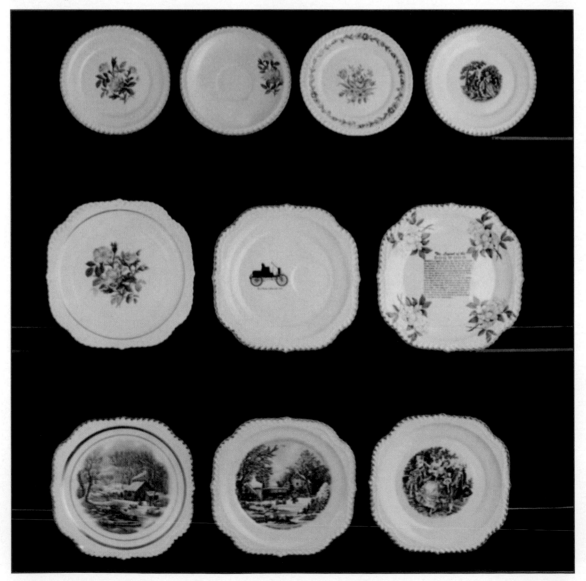

Cameoware

Cameoware had its beginning about 1935. George Bauer, formerly of the Bennett Pottery in Baltimore, and Harker's own design department are credited with Cameoware's engobe process designs. Many engobe process patterns were used on a variety of shapes.

One of the most popular engobe process designs was White Rose. The rolling pin was available with the design for a few cents more. The engobe process, as it was explained to me by Harker worker Jim Lange, is as follows:

"First, a rubber stamp would be cut in the desired pattern. The stamp had a cloth base and after repetitive uses would have to be discarded because fuzziness would appear on the fringe of the same.

This method was abandoned after a few years and sandblasting was the method used. When sandblasting was used, a copper mask was placed over the bisque and blasted with sand, leaving the imprint of the design.

In the original process, the rubber stamp was glued to the bisque, then dipped. When the glaze dried, the stamp would be removed with a tweezer by a worker and the process started again. Cameoware was not only hand-dipped but sent through a spray (dipping) machine.

The tops of the salt & pepper shakers and ends of rolling pins were covered with wax, so the glaze would not adhere, then stamp applied to the designated area, then dipped. The wax part was then sponged."

Blue and white seemed to be the most popular colors in Cameoware.

"Carv-Kraft was a name invented for Montgomery Ward to avoid the use of the name Cameo which was used on the regular department store trade. White Rose was a Montgomery Ward exclusive."

WHITE ROSE
carv-kraft
♦♦♦ BY HARKER

Harker Pottery backstamp.

Reprinted from a Montgomery Ward catalog, 1941.

Page 131

Row 1: Cameo Shell shape cup/saucer set, $10.00 – 15.00; White Rose drip jar, $18.00 – 25.00; pepper shaker, $10.00 – 15.00; Carv-Kraft White Rose cup/saucer set, $15.00 – 20.00.

Row 2: Shell shape 9" plate, $8.00 – 12.00; covered jugs, $20.00 – 30.00, $25.00 – 35.00, $30.00 – 40.00.

Row 3: White Rose teapot, $35.00 – 50.00; Cameo Rose covered casserole, $50.00 – 75.00; Cameo Rose pitcher (as is, cover missing), $25.00 – 30.00.

Row 4: Cameo Rose utility/serving plate 11¾", $15.00 – 20.00; Cameo Rose platter, $25.00 – 28.00; White Rose Carv-Kraft pie baker, $18.00 – 25.00.

1940s advertisement for Cameo.

Cameoware backstamps.

Row 1: Cameo Rose pink shakers, $18.00 – 25.00 set; Cameo Rose pink rolling pin, $50.00 – 75.00.

Row 2: Cameo Rose yellow fork, $20.00 – 25.00; yellow spoon, $20.00 – 25.00; large utility bowl, $35.00 – 50.00; Cameo ware advertising, $30.00 – 35.00.

Row 3: Cameo Rose gray plate, $20.00 – 25.00; Vine tan 7" plate, $8.00 – 12.00; Wheat plate, $5.00 – 10.00. Rooster plate called Engraved Rooster or Cock-O-the-Morn, $12.00 – 14.00.

Harker backstamps.

The Harker Holly plate was made prior to 1932 at the original plant on the river road in East Liverpool, Ohio. The Holly plate has an early backstamp.

White Clover was designed by the famous Russel Wright. There are many pieces to be found in this set. White Clover was made in Meadow Green, Coral Sand, Golden Spice and Charcoal. Russel Wright's signature is lightly incised in the back of the White Clover pieces. Not all of the pieces have the clover design. A 16-piece starter set sold for $9.95. The address, shown in the 1954 ad, was a mailing address only for the Harker plant.

Holly Christmas plate, 6", $15.00 – 20.00. White Clover designed by Russel Wright, $25.00 – 35.00.

Reprinted from *China, Glass & Tableware*, Clifton, New Jersey.

Russel Wright ad for a designed clock, $40.00 – 50.00.

Page 135

Row 1: Shakers (probably made by the Cronin China Company, Minerva, Ohio), Cherry decoration, $10.00 – 15.00 set; Harker Calico Tulip individual baking dish, $8.00 – 12.00; Calico Tulip creamer, $10.00 – 15.00; Calico Tulip sugar and cover, $15.00 – 25.00.

Row 2: Deco-Dahlia 6" utility jug, $12.00 – 15.00; Deco-Dahlia ashtray, 5¼", $12.00 – 15.00; Deco-Dahlia pie baker, $12.00 – 15.00; server, $12.00 – 15.00.

Row 3: Deco-Dahlia 12" utility tray, $18.00 – 22.00; Deco-Dahlia set of six custards in wire rack, complete set, $35.00 – 40.00.

Row 4: Cottage covered jar, $25.00 – 35.00; fork, $18.00 – 25.00; 8" plate, $10.00 – 17.00.

None of the shakers are marked and I am not totally convinced that all shakers with this shape belong to Harker. For now we will assume they are, but leave the door open for corrections.

Harker workers I talked to remember the pattern on Rows 2 and 3 as having an "Indian-sounding name," but were unable to recall what it was called.

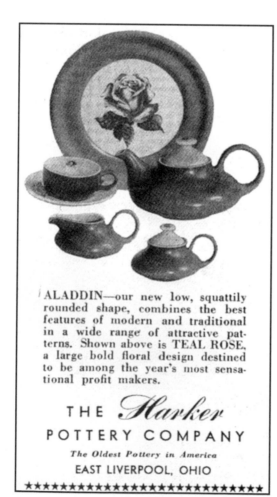

ALADDIN—our new low, squattily rounded shape, combines the best features of modern and traditional in a wide range of attractive patterns. Shown above is TEAL ROSE, a large bold floral design destined to be among the year's most sensational profit makers.

THE *Harker* POTTERY COMPANY

The Oldest Pottery in America

EAST LIVERPOOL, OHIO

1952 ad showing Teal Rose on Aladdin shape.

Countryside, Ivy, Birds and Flowers

Page 137

Row 1: All Countryside. Pepper shaker, $10.00 – 12.00; rolling pin, $90.00 – 150.00; server, $15.00 – 20.00.

Row 2: Countryside utility jug, Arches shape, $45.00 – 50.00; fork, $25.00 – 28.00; scoop, $75.00 – 100.00; large utility/mixing bowl, 10" across top, $35.00 – 50.00.

Row 3: Ivy decoration on Regal shape 7" pitcher, $25.00 – 30.00; Birds and Flowers on 8" Regal shape pitcher, $50.00 – 75.00.

Row 4: Ivy decoration on 12" utility server/tray, $15.00 – 20.00; Birds and Flowers 12" server/utility tray, $20.00 – 25.00.

1966 Harker ad.

Red Apple I & II

Red Apple was the name used by Harker workers for this decal. Again, for the sake of communication and ease of advertising, the small continuous decal will be referred to as Red Apple I. The larger decal will be referred to as Red Apple II. Dessert or cake sets were sometimes made up of utility plates, servers, and 6" dessert plates. The bowl, spoon, and eight small bowls were purchased as a berry set. It isn't known if it came as a berry set from the factory.

Prices reflect "as-is" pieces and pieces missing lids.

Page 139

Row 1: Red Apple II utility pitcher (lid missing), $15.00 – 18.00; custard marked Bakerite, $7.00 – 12.00; sugar (lid missing), $10.00 – 15.00; Red Apple I teapot, $15.00 – 25.00.

Row 2: Red Apple II. Swirl shape 9" bowl, $25.00 – 35.00; spoon, $15.00 – 18.00; berry bowl, $8.00 – 10.00; tile, $20.00 – 25.00.

Row 3: Red Apple II utility bowl, 10" across top, $25.00 – 35.00; Red Apple I large covered jug, complete with lid, $50.00 – 75.00.

Row 4: Red Apple II, utility serving tray, $25.00 – 30.00; server, $15.00 – 20.00; Red Apple I utility serving tray, $25.00 – 30.00.

The first pitcher on the top row, the utility pitcher, and one of the utility trays on the fourth row probably made up a batter set.

These pieces are shown to point out one decal's use on five and possibly more shapes. It was not uncommon for companies to get the best mileage possible out of what was on hand or was popular. This particular decal is found on lines by other companies.

Harker small plate and utility plate, Rust Tulip, marked Early American by Harker. Small plate $8.00 – 10.00; utility plate, $12.00 – 18.00.

Harker backstamp.

Page 141

Row 1: Rust Tulip decoration with red border, 6" plate, $6.00 – 8.00; Rust Tulip with gold trim oval 9" bowl, $10.00 – 15.00; Rust Tulip on gilded 6" plate, $6.00 – 8.00.

Row 2: Rust Tulip decoration on 12" utility tray, $12.00 – 18.00; Rust Tulip on Royal Gadroon shape plate, 8", $8.00 – 10.00.

Row 3: Pastel Tulip plate, 10", $10.00 – 12.00; Pastel Tulip cake plate, 11", $18.00 – 25.00.

Row 4: Pastel Tulip pie baker, $8.00 – 10.00; Hall jug with Pastel Tulip decoration, $35.00 – 40.00; utility/mixing bowl, $25.00 – 35.00.

Page 143
Row 1: Chesteron gray creamer, $10.00 – 15.00; gravy boat, $15.00 – 25.00; decaled creamer, $15.00 – 20.00.

Row 2: Ivy Vine platter, $15.00 – 18.00; 6" plate, $4.00 – 6.00; ashtray, $10.00 – 15.00; teapot, $40.00 – 50.00.

Row 3: Springtime 10" plate, gray shading around edge, $10.00 – 18.00; Springtime decal on teal shaded saucer, $4.00 – 6.00; Springtime decoration on 9" plate, $6.00 – 8.00.

Row 4: Teal 9" plate, "Paté sur Paté," $8.00 – 10.00; teal 6" plate, $4.00 – 6.00; teal 6" plate, $6.00 – 8.00; teal 9" plate, $8.00 – 10.00.

Harker Paté sur Paté backstamp. (See page 143)

HARKER CHESTERTON SERIES GENUINE AMERICAN IRONSTONE

Reminiscent of an English countryside...beautifully tailored and color coordinated to enhance any decor. Harker's underglaze process guarantees each piece oven proof, detergent proof, dishwasher safe.

Reprint from a Harker brochure.

Page 145
Row 1: Basket decoration on early creamer, $15.00 – 20.00; Shellridge sugar and cover, $15.00 – 20.00; Shellridge creamer, $15.00 – 20.00.

Row 2: Royal Rose decoration cake plate, $8.00 – 10.00; Royal Rose cake server, $12.00 – 15.00; cake/dessert plate, $6.00 – 8.00.

Row 3: Slender Leaf 8" plate, $6.00 – 8.00; Slender Leaf serving plate, $12.00 – 18.00.

Row 4: Rosettes plates. Left to right, $8.00 – 10.00; $6.00 – 8.00; $7.00 – 9.00; saucer, $4.00 – 6.00; bowl, $7.00 – 9.00.

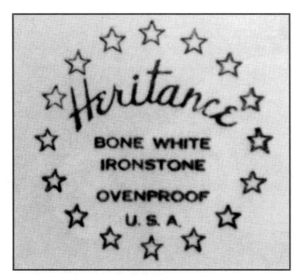

Heritance backstamp.

Reprinted from *China, Glass & Tableware*, Clifton, New Jersey.

Rawhide

Rawhide may be found in a variety of pieces. 1960s.

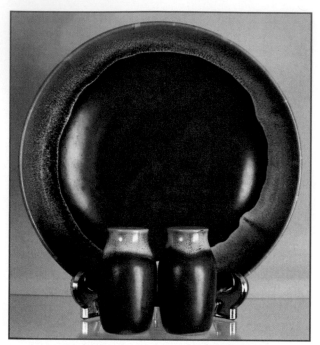

Stoneware shape and body. Rawhide large salad bowl, $6.00 – 8.00; salt/pepper set, $8.00 – 10.00.

Harker backstamps.

Row 1: Sun-Glo on Olympic shape (circa 1955) yellow plate, $10.00 – 15.00; Leaf and Flower plate made for Sears, Harmony House backstamp, $10.00 – 15.00.

Row 2: Laurelton shape made in green and beige (shown). Seems to be plentiful, $6.00 – 8.00; stoneware made in blue, pink, yellow, and white on pewter gray stoneware body. Sold in solid and mixed colors, $4.00 – 6.00.

Row 3: Provincial Wreath on white stoneware, Bouquet and Pine Cone plates, $6.00 – 8.00 each.

ROCKINGHAM-BROWN
DRIP GLAZE-IRONSTONE WARE

•

Oven-Dishwasher Proof

Complete Dinnerware Line, with
Specialty Pieces (34 items)

genuine
Quaker Maid
COOK
WARE
HARKER CHINA CO.
East Liverpool,
Ohio, USA
TRADEMARK

HARKER CHINA CO.
East Liverpool, Ohio   Established 1840

1960s trade publication ad.

BLUE DANE

Harker backstamps.

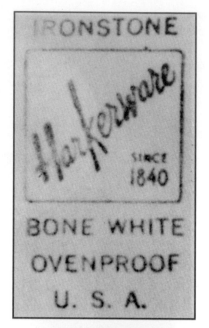

Harker backstamps.

Reproduction Rockingham Ware, 1960s

These Rockingham Ware pieces were developed in the sixties for the Harker Pottery Company by Norman Clewlow, Harker modeller. The pieces were intended as inexpensive gift shop items and were fashioned after Rockingham pieces popular in the mid-1800s at many American potteries.

The 1960s versions of the early Rockingham pieces are a soap dish, Toby pitcher, and a hound-handled pitcher and tumblers. Daniel Greatbach is credited with creating a similar design in America as early as 1839. The design had been used earlier in England. Many potteries were making a similar hound-handled pitcher in the mid-1800s, the most famous being made at Bennington, Vermont.

The Harker 1960s version of the hound-handled pitcher closely resembles the early version of the Harker-Taylor Rockingham pitcher.

Rockingham Ware is often erroneously referred to as Bennington. Bennington is a town in Vermont — a site of early American potteries. Rockingham Ware was named after the Duke of Rockingham whose potteries in England, it is said, first produced the ware.

Mugs, $10.00 – 20.00 each. Pitcher, $25.00 – 50.00.

1965 ad for Rockingham Ware. Left, gold mug, $20.00 – 25.00. Right, green mug, $20.00 – 25.00.

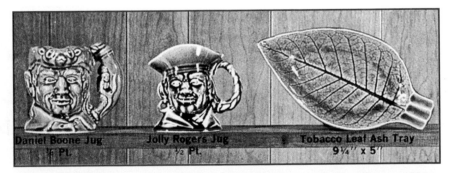

Daniel Boone Jug ¼ Pt.   Jolly Rogers Jug ½ Pt.   Tobacco Leaf Ash Tray 9¼" x 5'

Reproductions of early Harker Rockingham Ware. These pieces are generally marked "reproduction" and were made for the 1964 gift trade. Left to right, gold mug, $15.00 – 20.00; green, $20.00 – 25.00; Tobacco Leaf ashtray, gold or green, $20.00 – 30.00.

2 FOREST FLOWER

4 FOREVER YOURS

Shellridge China was made for you. American design and craftsmanship bring you quality at these reasonable prices. Made to be enjoyed every day, Shellridge is genuine translucent china. Graceful and sophisticated in the contemporary manner, with styling that makes it adaptable to any decor. Every piece is ovenproof and fully guaranteed against chipping, crazing or breaking for one full year. See manufacturer's liberal warranty certificate.

GARDEN TRAIL

1 Rich with the scent of mingled garden colors. Its graceful elegance makes it something special every day — every meal.

FOREST FLOWER

2 The breath of an enchanted forest glen brings a look of treasured beauty to your table. Subtle tones of warm light brown and yellow sparkle as the mist of spring.

LEAF SWIRL

3 Timeless grace and enduring beauty combine with the modern simplicity of this contemporary pattern. Its charm is highlighted by combined hues of greys, beige and browns that make it something special for every occasion.

FOREVER YOURS

4 A garland of Rosebuds with enduring beauty creates color loveliness for your sense of good taste. A pattern to be loved forever.

Reprint of a Harker brochure.

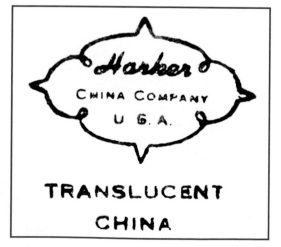

Harker backstamps.

Assorted Patterns on Shellridge Shape, Vitreous Casual China, Early Sixties

Row 1: Enchantment decoration on Shellridge China creamer, $15.00 – 20.00; Enchantment covered sugar, $15.00 – 20.00; Heritage covered sugar, $15.00 – 20.00; cup, no decoration, $8.00 – 10.00.

Row 2: Enchantment 6" plate, $6.00 – 8.00; 9" Enchantment plate, $8.00 – 10.00; Forest Flower bowl, $6.00 – 8.00.

Row 3: Leaf Swirl coffee server, $35.00 – 45.00; covered casserole with warmer base, no decoration, $30.00 – 35.00.

Vintage Pattern on Royal Gadroon Shape
Semi-Vitreous Pattern Made From 1947 – 1949

Row 1: Covered sugar, $12.00 – 15.00; cup/saucer set, $10.00 – 15.00; creamer, $10.00 – 15.00.

Row 2: 10" dinner plate, $8.00 – 10.00; 13" platter, $12.00 – 18.00.

Row 3: 8" flat soup, $8.00 – 10.00; sauce/fruit bowl, $8.00 – 10.00; 8" round vegetable bowl, $12.00 – 18.00.

Row 1: Colonial Lady covered cookie/utility jar, $35.00 – 45.00; bowl and cover, $30.00 – 35.00; batter set and tray: syrup and lid, $15.00 – 20.00; tray, $25.00 – 30.00; small batter jug and lid, $25.00 – 35.00.

Row 2: Rolling pin, $65.00 – 90.00; three-bowl set, $35.00 – 40.00.

Row 3: Cup/saucer set, $15.00 – 17.00; Modern Age teapot, $45.00 – 65.00; individual baker or custard, $8.00 – 10.00; creamer, $8.00 – 10.00; tab-handled bowl, $8.00 – 10.00.

Row 4: Table shakers set, $15.00 – 20.00; range set, "Drips" jar and salt & pepper shakers, $25.00 – 35.00 set; creamer, $8.00 – 12.00; sugar and cover, $10.00 – 15.00.

Hull Pottery Company

The A. E. Hull Pottery Co. was founded in 1905 and its main production was in the kitchenware field until 1918, at which time art ware was also added.

In 1950 the factory was completely destroyed by fire. It was rebuilt and in a year and a half was back in business. At this point the name was changed to Hull Pottery Company.

The most important line now in the factory is the House 'n Garden Serving Ware Line, originally conceived to be used primarily out-of-doors. However, within months of its introduction it was in the dining rooms of many homes.

House and Garden Serving Ware.

Crestone

Another OVENPROOF CREATION by Hull

Crestone, the newest casual serving-ware is saleable on sight! *Crestone's* refreshing Turquoise color and cascading white underglaze trim offers unusual eye-appeal. It's beautiful, it's ovenproof and sturdy and it's packed with special features. You'll love the uniquely designed deep-well saucers for cups and gravy boats, the comfortable platform handles, the easy-grip knobs that top interchangeable covers which invert and double for trivets. Over thirty sensibly-designed items such as *Crestone's* carafe are offered . . . and, at prices comparable to Hull's ever-popular Mirror Brown *House 'n Garden* line. Write for your *Crestone* and *House 'n Garden* folders today.

HULL POTTERY COMPANY
Crooksville, Ohio

Reprinted from *China, Glass & Tableware*, Clifton, New Jersey.

Illinois China Co.

Early information about Illinois China Co. is sketchy. The best information we have been able to piece together is as follows:

The Illinois China Co. was first located in Whitehall or Roodhouse, Illinois. (They are just a few miles apart.) Illinois China was moved to Lincoln, Illinois, by a group of Lincoln businessmen — James Shaw, William Coogan, and David Hart — in approximately 1919.

The first listing for the Illinois China Company in the Lincoln, Illinois, directory was 1920. The directory lists D. H. Hart, president, Will Houser, vice-president, and J. H. Smith, secretary-treasurer.

The entire plant was destroyed by fire in 1922. A new plant was built with insurance funds. A gas-fired kiln replaced the coal-fired kilns in 1935. Two and a half million dollars was spent on the plant and equipment after the 1946 Stetson purchase.

See Stetson history for examples of early Illinois ware.

Illinois China backstamp.

Jackson China Company

The Jackson China Company can be traced back to 1910 through the deed books at Brookville, Pennsylvania. It was first known as the Bohemian Pottery Company at Falls Creek, and the Bohemian Company specialized in crocks and flowerpots — until 1917 when the plant was bought by Harry Jackson.

The original investors and members of the original board were Mr. E. A. Fischel, Mr. H. W. Jackson, Mr. W. H. Cannon, Mr. J. Pifer, Mr. Frank Hahne, Sr., and Mr. Charles Dietz.

In the mid-1920s, an unnamed, disgruntled creditor of the original Bohemian Pottery hid in the bushes adjacent to the railroad tracks and shot and killed Mr. Jackson and Mr. Darden. The assailant then turned the gun on himself and committed suicide. Mr. Fischel had been delayed out of town on a business trip or he, too, would have been killed. Local interests continued the operation of the company. The plant was owned by Emanuel A. Fischer and was known as Jackson China Company from 1923 – 1946.

In 1946 all shares of stock were purchased by Philip R. Distillator. Mr. Distillator doubled the floor space in the manufacturing area, and added modern equipment in both forming and decorating. The work force more than doubled during this period of time. A decorating plant also operated in New York but was destroyed by fire in 1967.

The company made dinnerware for home use and marketed it under the name of Royal Jackson. Competition from foreign countries forced the company out of the dinnerware business.

In September 1976 Mr. Andrew Greystake, a British attorney and investment banking consultant, purchased the company.

Jackson China, Incorporated, as it is now known, produces institutional china for restaurants and hotels. It currently employs 375 people and provides a local payroll of $4,000,000.

The Jackson China, Incorporated, of Falls Creek, Pennsylvania, was recently acquired by Newman Industries of Bristol, England. Newman Industries is a large multi-national company involved in ceramics, engineering, and electric motors.

Jackson China backstamps.

Edwin M. Knowles Company

The Edwin M. Knowles Company was established in Chester, West Virginia, but moved to Newell, West Virginia, in 1900. The Knowles Company in later years was managed by a nephew, Fred B. Lawrence, Sr. Efforts to find a buyer for the plant in 1962 proved futile. In 1963, Robert Boyce and a Mr. Tuck, an area businessman, bought the Knowles real estate.

Edwin M. Knowles backstamps.

Edwin M. Knowles Medallion pitcher and bowl, part of a toilet set, $125.00 – 150.00 set.

Knowles Fruits 11" serving tray for batter set, $30.00 – 35.00; covered batter bowl, $35.00 – 40.00; covered syrup, $30.00 – 35.00; shaker, $15.00 – 18.00; pie server, $30.00 – 35.00.

Page 161

Row 1: Pink Pastel creamer, $14.00 – 16.00; Pink Pastel covered sugar, $15.00 – 18.00; Border Rim 4" fruit bowl, $4.00 – 6.00; Wildflower saucer, $4.00 – 6.00.

Row 2: Fruits shaker, $15.00 – 18.00; refrigerator covered jug, $35.00 – 40.00; saucer, $4.00 – 5.00; 6" plate, $4.00 – 6.00.

Row 3: Tulip time platter, $18.00 – 22.00; vegetable bowl, $15.00 – 20.00; 9" plate, $10.00 – 15.00.

Row 4: Knowles utility ware Tulip cookie jar; $55.00 – 65.00; Tulip pie baker, $25.00 – 30.00; Tulip Time decoration 4" fruit bowl, $2.00 – 3.00; Tulip Time 6" plate, $4.00 – 6.00.

SEQUOIA—OVENWARE ATTRACTIVE AS YOUR MOST COLORFUL DINNERWARE—YET OVEN-PROOF AND ACID-PROOF

A NEW kind of Ovenware—light-weight American Semi-Porcelain — brilliant design combining Yellow, Blue, Green and Tangerine with bright Red trimming in colorful gaiety on the Ivory White background. Attractive enough to grace the proudest table. Wards prices are 20 to 33 per cent lower than elsewhere and *Wards will replace any piece that cracks or crazes in the course of baking.* Save time, save dishwashing—bake, serve and store in the same dishes.

(A) 3-Piece Bowl Set $1⁴⁹
$1.95 Value! Hold 1, 2¾, 4 qts.
586 C 6991—Wt. 9 lbs. $1.49

(B) 3-Piece Range Set 79c
Salt and peppers. 4 in. high. Covered jar 4 by 3 in. high.
586 C 6984—Wt. 3 lbs. . . 79c

(C) Utility Pitchers 49c 18-oz.
586 C 6988—18-oz. 4¾ in. high. Ship. wt. 1 lb. 4 oz. 49c
586 C 6987—42-oz. 6 in. high.
Shipping weight 2 pounds 8 ounces. 69c

594 CBA

(D) Casserole and Tray $1⁰⁰ 1½-qt.
Usual $1.49 Value—Save 49c. Covered Casserole and matching 10-in. serving tray.
586 C 6980—1½-Qt. Casserole, 7⅝-in. diam., and Tray. Ship. wt. 6 lbs. 8 oz. $1.00
586 C 6981—2-Qt. Casserole, 8⅜-in. diam., and Tray. Ship. wt. 7 lbs. 8 oz. . . $1.19

(E) Custard Cups 12c ea.
So handy—you'll find dozens of uses for them. Capacity each, 5 oz. 3½-in. diam. Ship. wt. ea., 12 oz.; six, 4 lbs. 8 oz.
586 C 6989—Six.69c; Ea. 12c

(F) Beverage Pitcher 89c
New shape with ice lip for easy pouring. Large—70 oz. (2⅕ qts.) 7 in. high.
586 C 6985—Wt. 3 lbs. . . 89c

(G) Refrigerator Set $1¹⁹
Space saver—3 handy Jars each with cover. 4, 5 and 6-in. diams. Ship. wt. 5 lbs. 8 oz.
586 C 6992—Set. $1.19

(H) Refrigerator Ice Lip Jug 98c
Convenient—shaped to fit in refrigerator. 54-oz. ice-lip Jug with cover. 7½ in. high.
586 C 6986—Wt. 3 lbs. . . .98c

(J) Covered Butter Dish 79c
Keep butter covered and fresh. Tray 8½ by 4¾ in.
586 C 6990—Wt. 3 lbs. . . .79c

(K) 3-Piece Salad Set 98c
$1.39 Value—Save 41c at Wards. Big salad bowl, 9-in. diam. Matching fork and spoon.
586 C 6983—Wt. 4 lbs. . . .98c

(L) 3-Piece Waffle Set $1⁹⁸
Usual $2.49 Value! 42-oz. covered Batter Pitcher. 16-oz. covered Syrup Pitcher. Large attractive 11-in. serving Tray.
586 C 6993—Wt. 7 lbs. $1.98

11-Piece Set $2⁰⁹ *$2.98 Value*
Includes: 1½ qt. Covered Casserole and Plate; (D) Pie Plate and Server; (N) 6 Custard Cups; (E). Ship. wt. 18 lbs.
586 C 6995—11-Pc. . . $2.09

(M) Cookie Jar $1¹⁹ *$1.69 Value*
Big 4-qt. size. Snug inset cover keeps cookies fresh. Good size for baking beans. 7½ in. high.
586 C 6994—Wt. 4 lbs. 8 oz.$1.19

(N) Heat-Proof Pie Plate 29c Pie Plate
39c Value. Deep, even-heating. 9½-in. Pie Plate. Matching Server listed below. Ship. wt. 3 lbs.
586 C 6982—Pie Plate. . . .29c
586 C 6996—Server. Ship. wt. 12 oz. 19c

Sequoia ovenware from a late 1930s Wards catalog. The pitchers making up the batter set are also sold separately as utility pitchers. See item number C.

All pieces shown on this page are on the Yorktown shape. Yorktown was made in decorated and solid color pieces. All items are from the collection of John Moses.

Row 1: White coaster, $10.00 – 12.00; Cobalt blue shaker, $10.00 – 12.00; Mango Red shaker, $55.00 – 60.00; yellow shaker, $10.00 – 12.00; Mango Red teapot, $55.00 – 60.00; yellow shaker, $10.00 – 12.00; chop plate 10¾", $25.00 – 30.00.

Row 2: Penthouse decoration gravy, $20.00 – 25.00; Penthouse shaker, $10.00 – 12.00; Penthouse covered vegetable, $35.00 – 45.00; saucers, green, terra cotta, and pink, $4.00 – 5.00 each.

Row 3: 1939 chop plate made for World's Fair, $45.00 – 50.00; after-dinner cup, Picket Fence decoration, $20.00 – 25.00; teacup, $12.00 – 15.00; 10" dinner plate, Sailboats, $20.00 – 25.00.

All pieces shown on this page are the Deanna shape, also made in solid colors and decorated ware.

Row 1: Blue 9" plate, $10.00 – 15.00; yellow lug soup, $8.00 – 10.00; green coffee server, $45.00 – 50.00; red creamer, $10.00 – 15.00; pastel blue sugar and cover, $15.00 – 20.00.

Row 2: Pink Rose 10" dinner plate, $6.00 – 8.00; Plaid shaker, $6.00 – 8.00; Stripes coffee server, $45.00 – 50.00; Mini Flowers shaker, $6.00 – 8.00; 10" Wheat plate, $10.00 – 12.00.

Row 3: 8" Yellow Trim Poppy plate, $8.00 – 10.00; Daisies platter, $20.00 – 25.00; 7" Poppy plate, $6.00 – 8.00.

Row 1: Tia Juana decoration 8" flat soup, $18.00 – 20.00; shaker, $15.00 – 18.00; Bench decoration platter, $20.00 – 25.00; Bench cup, $8.00 – 10.00; Bench round vegetable bowl, $18.00 – 20.00.

Row 2: Sleeping Mexican 6" plate, $15.00 – 18.00; shaker, $15.00 – 18.00; after-dinner cup, $15.00 – 18.00; Tia Juana utility ware covered jar, $18.00 – 25.00; Tia Juana II (no gourds) cup, $12.00 – 15.00; saucer, $4.00 – 6.00.

Knowles used at least three Mexican motifs on the Deanna shape, the most common being Tia Juana showing a Mexican sitting in a doorway. There are two versions of Tia Juana.

Page 165

Row 1: Leaf Spray decoration covered sugar, $10.00 – 12.00; Wildflower decoration creamer, $10.00 – 12.00; Wildflower 4" fruit bowl, $4.00 – 6.00; 6" plate, $6.00 – 8.00.

Row 2: Golden Wheat platter, $12.00 – 15.00; Golden Wheat on Yorktown shape saucer, $4.00 – 6.00; Flower Spray platter, $12.00 – 15.00.

Row 3: Utility ware Tia Juana decoration refrigerator bowls, $8.00 – 10.00 each; Tia Juana covered batter jug, $55.00 – 65.00; covered syrup jug, $40.00 – 45.00; saucer, $4.00 – 6.00.

Row 4: Tia Juana utility serving tray/batter jug tray, $30.00 – 35.00; large utility/mixing bowl, $50.00 – 55.00.

Golden Wheat from a 1939 Wards catalog. Green Wheat by Knowles was introduced in 1936. "Inspired by, and complementing the Golden Wheat line, Green Wheat should prove a worthy companion." *1936 Crockery and Glass Journal.*

Golden Wheat $3.59 32-Pc.
USUAL $5.95 VALUE

A typically American pattern. Sprays of Golden Wheat in natural colors on charming modern shapes. Triple-selected first quality Ivory-White American Semi-Porcelain. Platters are round to harmonize with the other pieces. In the 95-Piece Set there are 2 round open vegetable dishes. Matching teapot and salt and peppers listed at right.

For Glassware and Cutlery, see Pages 320-324. Table linen on Pages 312-315. 95-Pc. set shipped in 2 packages. *All sets Mailable.* See Page 319 for composition of sets.

486 B 6251—32-Piece Set. Service for Six. Shipping weight 23 pounds............ **$3.59**

586 B 6255—Creamer and Sugar. Wt. 3 lbs......$1.18

486 B 6252—53-Piece Set. Service for Eight. Shipping weight 42 pounds.................. **$7.49**

386 B 6254—95-Piece Set. Service for Twelve. Shipping weight 76 pounds......... **$14.95**

586 B 6255—Extra Pieces—*State Article.* 6 (5 oz.) Cup Teapot. Shipping weight 3 pounds. 8 ounces..........98c
Salt and Peppers. Shipping weight 1 lb. 8 oz....Pr. 49c

586 B 6255—Open Stock on all but oval open vegetable dish. *State pattern and articles wanted*—see Page 319 for list of pieces and prices.

Knowles backstamp.

Knowles, Taylor & Knowles

Knowles, Taylor & Knowles can be traced to an 1853 beginning as Knowles and Harvey. Plant number 1 was on the corner of 6th and Walnut in East Liverpool. Isaac Knowles is listed as sole owner in 1867 in the same location. Knowles, Taylor & Knowles is listed from 1872 to 1929 when it became part of the American Chinaware Corporation. All plants are shown as being closed in 1931. (American Ceramic Society, 1945)

Knowles, Taylor & Knowles contributed much to the ceramic industry. Knowles, Laughlin, and Harker were competing for the introduction of white ware. Most sources credit Knowles with being the first to make white ware. All ware prior to that time made in the area had been yellow ware or Rockingham ware. Knowles also made the beautiful Lotus ware for a brief period of time.

Old Moss Rose decoration pitcher, marked "Knowles, Taylor, Knowles Ironstone China," $60.00 – 65.00.

Large Knowles, Taylor & Knowles platter, blue line border, "Rose Border," $25.00 – 30.00.

Knowles, Taylor & Knowles backstamp.

Knowles, Taylor & Knowles backstamp.

Homer Laughlin China Company

The Homer Laughlin China Company owes its origin to a two-kiln pottery in East Liverpool, Ohio, built in 1873 by Homer Laughlin and his brother Shakespeare Laughlin. The brother withdrew in 1879 and from that year until 1896 Homer Laughlin carried on the business as an individual enterprise. The Laughlin Pottery was one of the first white ware plants in the country. As early as 1876 Laughlin ware received the highest award at the Centennial Exposition held in Philadelphia in that year.

In 1889 William Edwin Wells came to East Liverpool to work with Homer Laughlin. Homer Laughlin incorporated his business at the end of 1896 and shortly thereafter sold his entire holdings to Mr. Wells and a Pittsburgh group headed by Mr. Marcus Aaron.

The new management, with Mr. Aaron as president and Mr. Wells as secretary-treasurer and general manager, soon abandoned the small River Road plant and expanded with two new and much larger plants at Laughlin Station, Ohio, three miles east of East Liverpool. They also purchased a third plant located close to the new ones and which had formerly been operated by another company. All of these plants were in operation by 1903. Very soon even these three plants were inadequate and in 1906 the first of the present factories, Homer Laughlin Plant 4, was built in Newell, West Virginia, just across the Ohio River from East Liverpool. In 1907 Plant 4 began operation. In 1913 Plant 5 was added.

The first revolutionary change in production methods came in 1923 when Plant 6 was built. The plant was equipped with continuous tunnel kilns instead of the old wasteful periodic kilns which had so long been the distinguishing landmark of potteries everywhere. The new type of plant was so successful that by 1929 two further tunnel kiln plants, Plant 7 (1927) and Plant 8 (1929), had been added. In 1929 the old East Liverpool factories fired their last ware and were withdrawn from production; meanwhile, in the years 1926 to 1934, the old kilns in Plant 4 and Plant 5 were replaced with modern tunnel kilns. Equally noteable with the change in firing methods has been the rapid mechanization of the potteries in more recent years. Spray glazing on high speed conveyors replaced many an old fashioned dipping tub. Conveyors moving at a slower speed reduced the wasted motion of men and materials. Even in the fashioning of the ware itself, mechanical jiggering came to substitute in large part for the traditional hand operation.

Quite as marked as the change in the production methods has been the change in the character of the ware produced.

In January 1930, after more than 40 years of magnificent work in the development and expansion of the business from a small riverside pottery in Ohio to the five great factories in West Virginia, and to a position of unquestioned leadership in its field, W. E. Wells retired from active director of the business and was succeeded by his son, Joseph Mahan Wells. Mr. Aaron became Chairman of the Board and his son, M. L. Aaron, succeeded him as President. Under the leadership of the younger Mr. Aaron and Mr. Wells, the company continued the manufacture of its previous successful wares and turned in addition to the creation of a series of new developments which have radically altered the type of domestic dinnerware in the American home.

First of these developments was the Wells Art Glaze line — Matt Green, Peach, and Rust, and later, Melon Yellow. Then followed the exquisite smooth texture, deep ivory glaze, known as Vellum, equally effective in undecorated ware and as a base for decorative treatments. The next outstanding step was in the field of cooking ware for table use — Ovenserve and Kitchen Kraft. From these most successful utilitarian wares, Homer Laughlin proceeded next to the creation of the most outstanding colored glaze lines of modern times, and in that field produced Fiesta, Harlequin, and Rhythm — wares which have become almost synonymous for colored glazes and have brought new cheer and warmth and joy to millions of Americans. A correlative development in the field of decorated ware resulted in the Homer Laughlin Eggshell line — thin, light, and graceful as no previous earthenware had been — ware of distinction and enduring quality. In 1959, the company started production of fine translucent table china, as well as a vitreous line for hotels and institutions.

Joseph M. Wells became Chairman of the Board and his son, Joseph M. Sells, Jr., assumed the position of

Executive Vice-President on January 1, 1960.

From the original two-kiln plant, employing about 60 people and producing about 6,000 pieces of dinnerware per day, the company grew to the employment of 2,500 people, the use of 1,500,000 square feet of production area, and the production of 360,000 pieces of dinnerware per day.

In 1976 approximately 1,200 employees produced over 46 million pieces of dinnerware with modern methods and equipment.

Dating Homer Laughlin China

The original trademark merely identifying the product as Laughlin Brothers appeared from the beginning in 1871 until around 1890. Unfortunately, reproductions are unavailable. The second trademark featuring the American Eagle astride the prostrate British Lion, signifying the end of the domination of the British in the dinnerware field in this country, was in use until around 1900. The third trademark, merely featuring the initials HLC with slight variations, has appeared on all dinnerware manufactured since that time and continues today.

Homer Laughlin Company, Newell, West Virginia.

In 1900 the trademark featured a single numeral identifying the month, a second single numeral identifying the year, and a numeral 1, 2, or 3 designating the point of manufacture as East Liverpool, Ohio.

In the period 1910 – 1920, the first figure indicated the month of the year, the next two numbers indicated the year, and the third figure designated the plant. No. 4 was "N," No. 5 was "N5," and the East End plant was "L."

A change was made for the period of 1921 – 1930. The first letter was used to indicate the month of the year such as "A" for January, "B" for February, and "C" for March. The next single digit number was used to indicate the year and the last figure for the plant.

For the period 1931 – 1940, the month was expressed as a letter, but the year was indicated with two digits. Plant No. 4 was "N," No. 5 was "R," Nos. 6 and 7 were "C," and No. 8 was listed as "P." During this period E-44R5 indicated May of 1944 and manufactured by Plant No. 5. The current trademark has been in use for approximately 70 years, and the numbers are the only indication of the year that items were produced.

The Homer Laughlin Company is one of the largest producers of restaurant ware and dinnerware in existence. It would be an impossible task to show all the ware turned out by Homer Laughlin in its many years of production. The Homer Laughlin Company is best known to collectors for its now famous Fiesta and Harlequin lines. Harlequin was reissued in 1978 and the plates are marked "Homer Laughlin 1978." (See marks). For more information, be sure to see *The Collector's Encyclopedia of Fiesta,* by Sharon and Bob Huxford, also published by Collector Books.

At left, a 1933 Homer Laughlin backstamp. Middle, early Homer Laughlin backstamps. At right, a 1980 Homer Laughlin backstamp.

Harlequin

ironstone dinnerware

Harlequin was introduced to the public in 1938 and lasted until the late 1950s, according to Sharon and Bob Huxford, authors of *Collector's Encyclopedia of Fiesta*. Solid colors on a lighter weight body, Harlequin was sold through the Woolworth stores.

Homer Laughlin backstamp.

The Homer Laughlin Compnay will long be remembered for its famous Fiesta colored ware introduced at a 1936 trade show. Fifty-four different items in four colors made up the original assortment. Different color assortments and items were added or dropped over the years.

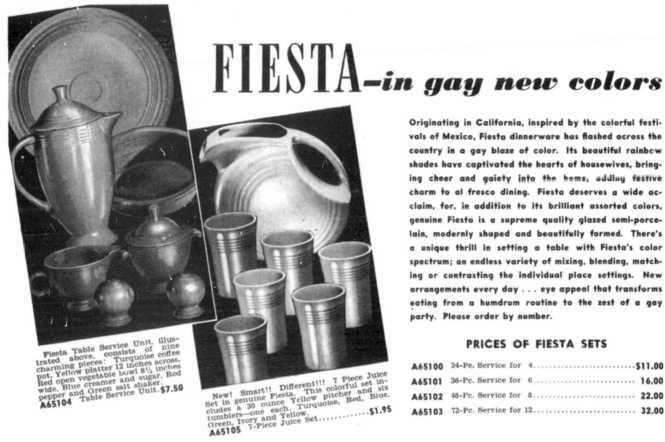

FIESTA—*in gay new colors*

Originating in California, inspired by the colorful festivals of Mexico, Fiesta dinnerware has flashed across the country in a gay blaze of color. Its beautiful rainbow shades have captivated the hearts of housewives, bringing cheer and gaiety into the home, adding festive charm to al fresco dining. Fiesta deserves a wide acclaim, for, in addition to its brilliant assorted colors, genuine Fiesta is a supreme quality glazed semi-porcelain, modernly shaped and beautifully formed. There's a unique thrill in setting a table with Fiesta's color spectrum; an endless variety of mixing, blending, matching or contrasting the individual place settings. New arrangements every day . . . eye appeal that transforms eating from a humdrum routine to the zest of a gay party. Please order by number.

Fiesta Table Service Unit, illustrated above, consists of nine charming pieces: Turquoise coffee pot, Yellow platter 12 inches across, Red open vegetable bowl 8½ inches wide, Blue creamer and sugar, Red pepper and Green salt shaker.
A65104 Table Service Unit–$7.50

New! Smart!! Different!!! 7 Piece Juice Set in genuine Fiesta. This colorful set includes a 30 ounce Yellow pitcher and six tumblers—one each, Turquoise, Red, Blue, Green, Ivory and Yellow.
A65105 7-Piece Juice Set.............$1.95

PRICES OF FIESTA SETS

A65100	24-Pc. Service for 4	$11.00
A65101	36-Pc. Service for 6	16.00
A65102	48-Pc. Service for 8	22.00
A65103	72-Pc. Service for 12	32.00

Fiesta ad, 1938.

Fiesta backstamp.

Amberstone

A 1967 Sheffield Amberstone order blank lists the following pieces: dinner plate, dessert dish, bread and butter plate, coffee cup, saucer, vegetable bowl, covered sugar, creamer, 13" platter, large soup plate, ashtray, salt & pepper, salad plate, soup/cereal bowl, covered casserole, sauce boat, relish tray, coffee server, tea server, covered butter, round serving platter, jumbo salad bowl, covered jam jar, serving pitcher, jumbo mug, and pie plate. Only pieces large enough to accommodate the design carry it; other pieces are plain. Some of the hollow ware pieces are marked "Fiesta."

Page 173

Row 1: Amberstone quarter lb. butter, $30.00 – 35.00; gravy/sauce boat, $25.00 – 30.00; salt and pepper shakers, $12.00 – 15.00 set; cup, $5.00 – 6.00.

Row 2: Saucer, $2.00 – 4.00; sauce/fruit dish, $3.00 – 4.00; gravy/sauce boat liner, $18.00 – 20.00; 6" dessert plate, $4.00 – 6.00.

Row 3: Platter, $12.00 – 16.00; coffee server, $45.00 – 55.00; plate, $6.00 – 8.00.

Row 4: Soup bowl, $5.00 – 8.00; handled serving tray, $25.00 – 30.00.

1930 – 1931 Wards catalog.

Homer Laughlin backstamp.

Row 1: All Homer Laughlin Wells line. Red Stripe sugar and cover, $35.00 – 45.00; green platter, $35.00 – 45.00; Wells Red Stripe butter dish, $100.00 – 125.00; Red Stripe creamer, $25.00 – 35.00.

Row 2: Tab-handled green nappy, may be Nautilus shape with Wells green glaze, unusual, $35.00 – 50.00; Hollyhock decoration coffee server and cover, $125.00 – 200.00; green glaze covered syrup, $50.00 – 75.00.

Row 3: Wells green glaze cup, $10.00 – 12.00; Rose teapot, $175.00 – 200.00; Rust after dinner cup/saucer set, $25.00 – 35.00; Palm Tree decoration on 9" plate, $35.00 – 40.00.

ITEMS AVAILABLE

1 Tea Cup	8 Coupe Soup 8"	15 Sauceboat	22 Water Jug
2 Tea Saucer	9 Cereal Soup	16 Casserole Cov'd	POPULAR SETS—ADDITIONAL ITEMS OBTAINABLE FROM OPEN STOCK
3 Plate 10"	10 Fruit 5½"	17 Sugar Cov'd	
4 Plate 9"	11 Nappie 9"	18 Cream	20 Pc. B SERVICE FOR 4 WITH 9" PLATES
5 Plate 8"	12 Platter 11½"	19 Salt Shaker	20 Pc. AT SERVICE FOR 4 WITH 10" PLATES
6 Plate 7"	13 Platter 13½"	20 Pepper Shaker	32 Pc. D SERVICE FOR 6 WITH 9" PLATES
7 Plate 6"	14 Pickle	21 Tea Pot Cov'd	53 Pc. C SERVICE FOR 8 WITH 10" PLATES

THE HOMER LAUGHLIN CHINA COMPANY, NEWELL, WEST VIRGINIA

Advertising brochure for American Provincial.

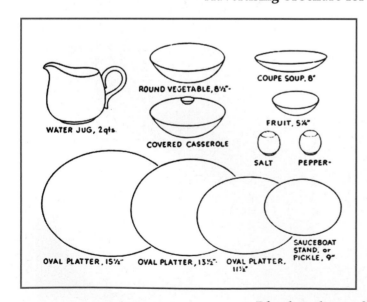

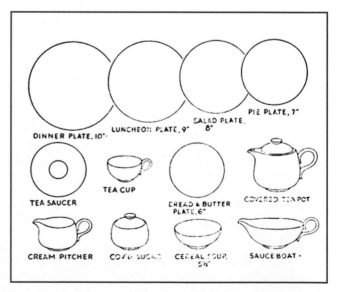

Rhythm shapes from brochure.

Rhythm Shape

Row 1: Forest green sugar and cover, $18.00 – 20.00; Chartreuse creamer, $10.00 – 14.00; Harlequin yellow creamer, $10.00 – 14.00; burgundy teapot and cover, $55.00 – 65.00; gray cup, $6.00 – 8.00; Chartreuse saucer, $2.00 – 4.00.

Row 2: Chartreuse plate, 10", $10.00 – 12.00; gravy/sauce boat, $12.00 – 15.00, burgundy cereal/soup dish, 5½", $8.00 – 10.00; gray sauce/fruit dish, 5¼", $5.00 – 8.00.

Row 3: Gray shaker, $6.00 – 8.00; yellow shaker, $6.00 – 8.00; American Provincial 7" plate, $6.00 – 8.00; decaled teapot and cover (decoration not known), $30.00 – 35.00; creamer, not Rhythm but Cavalier shape, $12.00 – 14.00.

Page 179

Yellowstone shape, assorted decals.

The Yellowstone shape was introduced in 1927. The shape was used for many years and was decorated with many different patterns over the years.

Row 1: Sugar (no lid), $6.00 – 8.00; gravy/sauce boat, $12.00 – 15.00; sugar/cover, $16.00 – 18.00; plate, $6.00 – 8.00.

Row 2: 10" plate, $8.00 – 10.00; 9" plate, $6.00 – 8.00; cereal/soup bowl, $4.00 – 6.00; fruit/sauce bowl, $3.00 – 4.00.

Row 3: Platter, $15.00 – 18.00; larger platter, $18.00 – 22.00.

Row 4: 7" plates, assorted decorations, $6.00 – 8.00 each.

A 1926 wholesale catalog showing "the popular new octagonal shape" in the Raymond pattern. A variety of treatments and decals was used on the Yellowstone octagonal shape over a period of many years. A colorful peacock is found on some pieces of Homer Laughlin ware. The art glazes are marked "Wells."

Homer Laughlin "Wells" backstamp.

A 1927 wholesale catalog reprint showing the Rosetta decoration on the Yellowstone shape.

Yellowstone – new shape for 1927. Advertisement from 1927 *Pottery, Glass & Brass Salesman.*

Row 1: All Yellowstone octagonal shape Max-i-cana decoration (not an official name). Gravy/sauce boat, $55.00; casserole and cover, $135.00; Jade shape butter and cover, $150.00.

Row 2: All Max-i-cana decoration on Yellowstone shape. Cup/saucer set, $35.00; platter, $55.00; egg cup, $60.00; sugar and cover, $50.00.

Row 3: Pink Rose teapot, $30.00; flat soup, $12.00; butter and cover, $25.00; decaled creamer, $12.00.

From the collection of John Moses.

Page 183

Row 1: Republic shape, sugar and cover, $14.00 – 18.00; Republic saucer, $4.00 – 6.00; Georgian Eggshell sugar and cover, $12.00 – 16.00; Georgian Eggshell shape sugar and cover, decoration #G-3466, $14.00 – 18.00; Republic shape, Priscilla decoration creamer, $12.00 – 14.00; Republic shape 6" plate, $4.00 – 6.00.

Row 2: Liberty shape 10" plate, $8.00 – 10.00; Liberty shape 6" plate, $4.00 – 6.00; Nautilus Eggshell decoration #N-1577, Ferndale flat soup, $12.00 – 15.00; Nautilus Eggshell 10" plate, decoration #N-1594 Pastel Tulip, $12.00 – 14.00.

Row 3: Kitchen Kraft decoration KK-436 pie baker, $20.00 – 25.00; Nautilus Regular shape Colonial decoration on Nautilus Regular shape creamer, Colonial decoration, $12.00 – 15.00; saucer, $2.00 – 4.00; Liberty shape teapot, Dogwood decoration, $35.00 – 40.00.

Row 4: Greenbriar decoration #G-3370 on Georgian Eggshell 10" plate, $8.00 – 10.00; Greenbriar decoration #G-3499 Georgian gravy/sauce boat, $12.00 – 15.00; liner, $10.00 – 12.00; 10" plate, $10.00 – 12.00.

Homer Laughlin backstamp.

A variety of marks used over a period of years by the Homer Laughlin Company, Newell, West Virginia.

All pieces are from the 1935 – 1945 period with assorted decals.

Row 1: Decoration #K-303 on small Kitchen Kraft bowl, $15.00 – 18.00; Spring Wreath decoration #A-C186 mixing/utility bowl, $35.00 – 45.00; Spring Wreath covered casserole, $35.00 – 40.00.

Row 2: Starflower decoration on Kitchen Kraft pie baker, $20.00 – 25.00; Spring Wreath serving/utility tray, $30.00 – 35.00.

Row 3: Kitchen Bouquet decoration on Kitchen Kraft pie baker, $20.00 – 25.00; lid only, $12.00 – 15.00.

Row 4: Starflower decoration on Kitchen Kraft mixing/utility bowl, $30.00 – 35.00; Pueblo decoration on Kitchen Kraft platter, $15.00 – 20.00.

Priscilla

Page 187
All Priscilla decoration on Nautilus Eggshell shape.

Row 1: Sugar and cover, $18.00 – 20.00; saucer, $2.00 – 4.00; creamer, $12.00 – 15.00.

Row 2: Pie baker, $25.00 – 30.00; 9" plate, $10.00 – 12.00; 8" plate, $8.00 – 10.00.

Row 3: Covered casserole, $30.00 – 35.00; mixing/utility bowl, $25.00 – 30.00.

Row 4: Coffee server, $35.00 – 40.00; large mixing/utility bowl, $35.00 – 40.00.

Priscilla decoration on Nautilus Eggshell shape teapot, $35.00 – 40.00.

Homer Laughlin Priscilla backstamp.

Page 189

Row 1: All Century shape. Arizona saucer, $12.00 – 14.00; Conchita sugar (lid missing), $8.00 – 10.00; if complete, $45.00; Conchita creamer, $40.00; Conchita cup, $35.00; Arizona fruit/sauce bowl, $40.00.

Row 2: All Century shape. Hacienda decoration 6" bread & butter plate, $15.00; Hacienda saucer, $10.00; English Garden saucer, $12.00; Gold Lace 6" bread & butter plate, $3.00.

Row 3: All 9" luncheon plates. Briar Rose, $25.00; Fruit Medley, $15.00; Mexicana, $30.00.

Row 4: Century shape Hacienda decoration platter, $50.00; Mexicana platter, $50.00.

English Garden decal on square Century shape as offered in a 1933 Sears catalog.

Virginia Rose Shape

The Virginia Rose shape was estimated by Mr. Ed Carson of the Homer Laughlin Company to have been made from 1935 to 1959 with as many as 150 different decals used on this blank. Most collectors refer to this pattern as Virginia Rose. Many other serving and dinnerware pieces are available in Virginia Rose, a favorite with collectors.

Page 191

Row 1: Virginia Rose shape, called JJ59 by collectors, gravy, $14.00 – 16.00; salt and pepper shakers, no price established, very hard to find; egg cup, $100.00 – 105.00; creamer, $12.00 – 14.00; sugar and cover, $16.00 – 18.00.

Row 2: Virginia Rose shape, JJ59 covered butter, $105.00 – 110.00; pitcher, $225.00 – 250.00; covered vegetable, $115.00 – 125.00.

Row 3: Jade shape covered butter, $105.00 – 110.00; all JJ59 decoration: 9" plate, $8.00 – 10.00; cup/saucer set, $12.00 – 14.00; flat soup, $14.00 – 16.00; pie baker, $35.00 – 40.00.

Row 4: Mixing bowls, set of three, $112.00 – $127.00; 6" bowl, $40.00 – $45.00; 8" bowl, $30.00 – $35.00; 10" bowl, $42.00 – $47.00; pickle dish/gravy boat liner, $30.00 – 32.00; large platter, $22.00 – 28.00.

1950s advertisement for Homer Laughlin China.

An assortment of decorations on the Virginia Rose shape.

Row 1: Three 6" plates, $4.00 – 6.00 each; saucer, $2.00 – 3.00.

Row 2: 6" plate, $4.00 – 6.00; saucer, $2.00 – 3.00; saucers, $2.00 – 4.00 each; creamer, $16.00 – 18.00.

Row 3: Large plates, $10.00 – 12.00 each; small plate, $6.00 – 8.00.

Row 4: Bowl with Fruit decoration, $20.00 – 25.00; platter with green trim, $15.00 – 20.00; undecorated flat soup, $6.00 – 8.00.

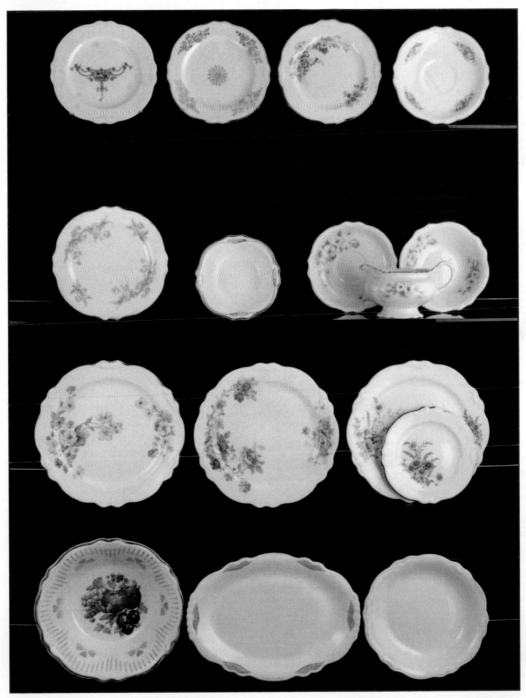

Epicure

Homer Laughlin's newest and smartest dinnerware for casual dining! Its superb styling with textured glazes in charming colors of Dawn Pink, Snow White, Charcoal Gray and Turquoise Blue creates an incomparable table setting. Sturdy . . . Multi-purpose . . . Ovenproof . . . Meeting America's demand for function and beauty at modest prices.

Full color National advertising starting in May issues of leading consumer magazines will bring pre-sold customers to your store.

Plan now to meet the demand with EPICURE — The most salesworthy dinnerware 1955 will see.

The Homer Laughlin China Co.
NEWELL, WEST VIRGINIA

Homer Laughlin China Company 1955 advertisement for its new Epicure shape.

Row 1: Jubilee/Skytone shape, Stardust decoration sugar and lid, $14.00 – 16.00; salt and pepper set, $8.00 – 10.00 each; gravy, $14.00 – 16.00; Kraft Blue shape, also with Stardust decoration, $16.00 – 18.00.

Row 2: Jubilee/Skytone shape, Stardust decoration 10" plate, $8.00 – 10.00; 7" plate, $8.00 – 10.00; saucer, $2.00 – 4.00; 6" plate, $4.00 – 6.00.

Row 3: Jubilee/Skytone covered casserole, $30.00 – 35.00; fast-stand gravy boat, $15.00 – 20.00.

Homer Laughlin Skytone backstamp.

Briar Rose is only one of the many decorations found on Homer Laughlin's Century shape. Riviera (colored glazes) was introduced in 1938, and Sharon and Bob Huxford, in their *Collector's Encyclopedia of Fiesta*, tell us it was a limited line and sold exclusively by the Murphy Company. Riviera colors are blue, light green, red, yellow, and ivory.

From a 1933 Sears catalog.

All Homer Laughlin Century shape colored-glaze ware called Riviera.

Page 197
Row 1: Blue bowl, $10.00 – 15.00; red sugar and cover, $30.00 – 40.00; yellow sugar and cover, $30.00 – 40.00; yellow fruit/sauce bowl, $10.00 – 15.00.

Row 2: Riviera 7" blue plate, $8.00 – 10.00; tangerine red 7" plate, $8.00 – 10.00; blue creamer, $15.00 – 20.00; yellow 7" plate, $8.00 – 10.00; green 7" plate, $8.00 – 10.00.

Row 3: Riviera blue 9" plate, $20.00 – 25.00; tangerine red 9" plate, $20.00 – 25.00; yellow 9" plate, $20.00 – 25.00; green 9" plate, $20.00 – 25.00.

Row 4: Blue Riviera cup/saucer set, $20.00 – 30.00; yellow meat platter, $30.00 – 40.00; yellow cup/saucer, $20.00 – 30.00.

Organdy Pastels after-dinner set made by the Homer Laughlin China Company on the Swing shape. Cup/saucer, $18.00 – 22.00 set; plates, $6.00 – 8.00 each.

Advertisement for Organdy Pastels on the Swing shape.

Nautilus Eggshell Shape
Circa 1935 – 1955

Row 1: Apple Blossom, decal number N-1627. Top left, platter, $20.00 – 25.00; covered casserole, $40.00 – 45.00.

Row 2: Gravy boat, $18.00 – 25.00; liner, $12.00 – 15.00; sugar and cover, $15.00 – 20.00.

Row 3: Fruit dish, $4.00 – 6.00; dinner plate, $20.00 – 22.00; flat soup, $12.00 – 15.00; cup/saucer set, $12.00 – 15.00 set.

The Homer Laughlin China Company is one of the largest producers of American-made restaurant and dinnerware. It would not be possible to picture all of the ware this gigantic company has produced over the years.

Homer Laughlin Eggshell backstamps.

Page 201 – Brittany shape, assorted similar decorations.

Row 1: 9" plate, $6.00 – 8.00; saucer, $2.00 – 4.00; small platter, $12.00 – 15.00.

Row 2: Brittany shape 10" plate, $10.00 – 12.00; sugar and cover, $15.00 – 18.00; Brittany cup with blue decoration, $6.00 – 8.00; saucer, $2.00 – 4.00.

Row 3: Debutante shape plate, Leaping decoration, $8.00 – 10.00; Brittany 10" plate, $6.00 – 8.00; Debutante shape plate, Berry Vine decoration, $6.00 – 8.00.

Row 4: Brittany 9" plate, yellow/black decoration, $6.00 – 8.00; Empress shape plate with Bluebird decoration, $16.00 – 20.00; Brittany shape plate, Green Star, $8.00 – 10.00.

Catalog reprints showing Homer Laughlin dinnerware.

Homer Laughlin backstamp.

Row 1: Homer Laughlin Orleans shape, Silver Stripe sugar (lid missing), $10.00 – 12.00; if complete, $16.00 – 18.00; Silver Stripe creamer, $16.00 – 18.00; Empress gravy/sauce boat, decoration #E-7505, $16.00 – 20.00; liner, $10.00 – 12.00; Nautilus Regular Old Curiosity Shop creamer, $14.00 – 16.00.

Row 2: Century shape 9" plate, Columbine decoration, $10.00 – 12.00; Republic shape, Bluebird decoration, $8.00 – 10.00; Empress shape platter, Bluebird decoration, $30.00 – 35.00.

Row 3: Debutante shape calendar plate, $5.00 – 7.00; Brittany shape bowl, $4.00 – 6.00; Empress shape plate, $4.00 – 6.00.

Row 4: Brittany shape plate, Apple and Pear, $12.00 – 14.00; Rhythm shape plate, rose with gold trim, $8.00 – 10.00; Brittany shape plate, Kitchen Window, $6.00 – 8.00.

Leigh and Crescent

A listing for the Crescent Pottery first appeared in the Alliance, Ohio, city directory in 1921 – 1922 with Charles L. Sebring as president. Crescent was still listed in the 1927 – 1928 directory with the name of Frank Sebring, and in 1929 – 1930 with the name of Leigh Potters, Inc. in parentheses. The pottery was listed as Leigh Potters, Inc. with Frank Sebring, chairman, Charles Sebring, president, Frank Sebring, Jr., vice president, Charles Baker, secretary, and George Stanford, general manager. The last listing for the pottery was 1938.

Frank Sebring had retained the molds from The Tritt China Plant in Niles, Ohio (See Universal Pottery). Strangely enough, when the Tritt operation was reopened, the Niles Tritt plant was also named Crescent. Its backstamp was also the half-moon shape. So, for at least a short period of time, there were two Crescent plants — one in Niles, Ohio, and the other in Alliance, Ohio. There are some remembrances about an infringement suit involving the Crescent name. At any rate, The Crescent China Co. in Niles changed its name in 1923 to Atlas China Company (See Universal Pottery).

The Leigh Pottery building was sold to Alliance Manufacturing.

A 1940 article from the *Alliance Review* reports that Charles Leigh Sebring was leaving Sebring to be the design manager of Edwin M. Knowles China Company, then the third largest in the United States. Charles L. Sebring was also associated with Limoges and Salem China Companies and at that time (1940) was chairman of the United States Potters Association.

Catalog advertisement for Housetops.

The Sienna ware Crescent was a trademark of ware made at Alliance, Ohio. The Crescent China Company in Niles also used the half-moon mark at least for a short period of time.

1930s ads for Leigh dinnerware.

Leigh Ware was named after the owner of Leigh Potteries of Alliance, Ohio. In a 1929 article on Leigh Ware by Alden Welles in *The Crockery and Glass Journal*. C. L. Sebring is said to be "one of the most progressive forces in the business today." (1929) The color of Leigh Ware is achieved by the umbertone body and not the glaze. A unique innovation indeed! At the time of the 1929 article, it was pointed out that Leigh Ware had not long been on the market. Gale Turnbull is credited with designing the ware under the direction of technical supervisor Joseph Palin Thorley. The dinner service is described as conservative with the details of bundles, decorative knobs and the "setback" form of handles.

The "novel treatment of the patterns" on the creamy tan background is what sets Leigh Ware apart from all other dinnerware of its time. Pastel borders of two or more pastel colors, "artful placing" of decoration, and a silver trim (actually platinum and white gold) around the edges were the three types of decorations used.

Leigh (according to the same article) had produced an art ware line comprised of "lamp bases, vases, flower bowls and fruit bowls, wall pockets, bookends, etc."

Leigh backstamps.

Be sure to read Universal's early history dating back to the early 1920s in Niles, Ohio. It is possible that two plants called Crescent were in operation at the same time, if but briefly, circa 1922 – 1923. The same backstamp (half-moon) was used both at Niles and Alliance.

Page 207

Row 1: Crescent 7" liner plate for cream soup, Tulip decoration, $10.00 – 12.00; sugar with cover, Tulip, $25.00 – 30.00; Tulip cup/saucer set, $18.00 – 20.00.

Row 2: Crescent tile in Farberware frame, Basket decoration, $18.00 – 20.00; Leigh cup, Mayfair decoration, $8.00 – 10.00; Leigh Indian Tree decoration tile in Farberware frame, $18.00 – 20.00.

Row 3: Leigh Petit Point border casserole and cover, $45.00 – 50.00; Leigh Fuchsia ice bucket with Farberware handle and rim, $50.00 – 55.00.

Row 4: Leigh 9" plate, Mayfair decoration, $14.00 – 16.00; Leigh single plate tidbit tray, Green Wheat, $25.00 – 28.00.

Leigh Potters Fuchsia candy dish with metal trim, $30.00 – 35.00.

Row 1: All Leigh ware. Modern Tulip decoration cup/saucer, $18.00 – 24.00 set; 9" plate, $15.00 – 18.00; candy dish with Farberware handle and rim, $18.00 – 22.00.

Row 2: Modern Tulip bowl with metal rim, $15.00 – 20.00; warming food bowl, $25.00 – 30.00.

Row 3: Tidbit plate, $25.00 – 28.00; different style tidbit plate, $25.00 – 30.00.

Row 1: Fuchsia decoration 13" platter, $30.00 – 35.00; Fuchsia teapot, $55.00 – 60.00; gravy boat, $25.00 – 30.00.

Row 2: Leigh ware 9" plate, Iris Bouquet decoration, $18.00 – 20.00; 7" plate, $14.00 – 16.00; 5" fruit/sauce dish, $10.00 – 12.00; cream soup, $25.00 – 30.00.

Row 3: Manhattan demitasse cup/saucer, $15.00 – 20.00 set; 1-lb. butter dish/cover, $75.00 – 95.00; creamer, $15.00 – 20.00, sugar and cover, $20.00 – 25.00.

Limoges China Company

The Limoges China Company was located in Sebring, Ohio, and was one of the many potteries owned by the Sebring family. The Sebrings are credited with founding two towns — Sebring, Ohio, for the purpose of opening potteries, and Sebring, Florida, probably for the purpose of rest and recreation — all done with $7,000 of borrowed money.

The Limoges China Company was opened in approximately 1901 by F. A. Sebring, one of the Sebring brothers. Mr. Sebring's plan for the Limoges China company was to produce "thin porcelain products" like European ware. Highly trained help was brought from Europe and materials were imported as well.

The third year of business for Limoges was a disastrous one, as a fire destroyed equipment and is said to have indirectly been the cause of the untimely death of the European ceramic expert.

Limoges China Company was completely renovated and shut down only briefly. The reopening was under the supervision of one of the younger Sebring brothers and semi-porcelain/earthenware was produced. The first of the tunnel kilns and decals are said to have made their debut there, according to Limoges. Limoges also claimed the first "industrial ceramic laboratories" with graduate ceramic engineers, and was one of the first companies to have a full-time artist and designer. Quite an impressive list of claims of "firsts."

In 1946, there was a campaign to sell retail Limoges ware only through stores bearing the name "House of American Limoges." This was probably to overcome the charges made by the Haviland people of Limoges, France. For this reason, "American" became a part of Limoges' advertising.

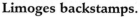

Limoges backstamps.

Mt. Clemens Pottery

The Mt. Clemens Pottery had been owned by the S. S. Kresge Company since 1920. S. S. Kresge (now K-Mart) decided to sell the operation in 1965 and apply proceeds to their rapidly expanding operations. Mr. David Chase of Hartford, Connecticut, was the buyer and Mr. Sam Sabin became associated in a sales capacity. Mr. Sabin retained ownership of the Sabin China Company in McKeesport, Pennsylvania. The Sabin-McKeesport operation was destroyed by fire in 1979 and Mr. Sabin and his son David transferred their operation to Mt. Clemens where they have a partnership arrangement with Mr. Chase. They now decorate their ware in the old Mt. Clemens facilities and consider the possibility of actually manufacturing dinnerware.

Row 1: All Mt. Clemens yellow glaze and Old Mexico decoration. Alara shape plate, $20.00 – 25.00; flat soup, $18.00 – 20.00; cup, $10.00 – 14.00; vegetable bowl, $35.00 – 40.00.

Row 2: Stetson decorated Alara shape creamer, Posies, $8.00 – 10.00; Old Mexico decoration creamer, $18.00 – 20.00; Posies sugar (no lid), $10.00 – 12.00; Old Mexico sugar (no lid), $15.00 – 18.00; Stetson decorated sugar, Veggies, $8.00 – 10.00.

Row 3: Stetson decorated Petit Point Rose plate, $6.00   8.00; sugar (no lid), $6.00 – 8.00; creamer, $10.00 – 12.00; cup, $6.00 – 8.00; Springtime decoration flat soup, $8.00 – 10.00.

Page 213
All California Poppy decoration on Mt. Clemens Toulon shape.

Row 1: Creamer, $8.00 – 10.00; gravy/sauce boat, $15.00 – 18.00; sugar (no lid), $8.00 – 10.00.

Row 2: 7" plate, $6.00 – 8.00; covered vegetable bowl, $25.00 – 30.00; 9" plate, $10.00 – 12.00.

Row 3: Small platter, $14.00 – 18.00; large platter, $18.00 – 22.00.

MOUNT CLEMENS POTTERY COMPANY. The success of "Sierrastone" dinnerware is based on the appeal, to many homemakers, of solid-colored table appointments. The plate is a cross between a coupe and a rim shape; the cup is in the Empire shape. A 53-piece set is priced to retail for $19.29.

From *China, Glass & Tablewares*, 1967.

MOUNT CLEMENS POTTERY COMPANY. Introduced last fall, this coupe-shaped fluted white ironstone dinnerware comes with over 100 pattern choices; just right for use with bright place mats and napkins. A 47-piece service retails for about $11.

From *China, Glass & Tablewares*, September 1966.

Paden City Pottery

Red cooking ware fired in one upright kiln was the first ware made at the Paden City Pottery in Paden City, West Virginia. The Paden City Pottery was founded in 1907 by George Lasell.

Vases, teapots, and bulb bowls were new items at the 1922 Ft. Pitt Hotel Show. The mahogany finish was reported as being a late development of Paden City Pottery. Tea sets in jet and mahogany were also offered in 1922 as was kitchenware. By December 1923 Paden City's plain white semi-porcelain dinnerware in the Ransom shape was ready for delivery.

Paden City Pottery is credited with originating the underglaze decal and the Caliente colored glaze. By 1949 Paden City Pottery had six tunnel kilns and personnel totaling 800. Paden City Pottery closed in the 1950s.

Page 215
Row 1: Regina shape 9" plate, Spring Blossom decoration, $12.00 – 14.00; cup, $8.00 – 10.00; Acacia Flower casserole in Manning Bowman frame, $20.00 – 24.00; Regina shape 9" plate, Touch of Black decoration, $10.00 – 12.00.

Row 2: Regina shape 6" plate, Jonquil decoration, $4.00 – 6.00; Minion shape serving plate, American Beauty decoration, $12.00 – 15.00; American Beauty after-dinner cup/saucer set, $12.00 – 15.00.

Row 3: Novelty cartoon 6" plates, cartoons by Peter Arno, $8.00 – 10.00 each; cobalt colored ware on Regina shape, $16.00 – 18.00; Tangerine 6" plate, $12.00 – 15.00.

Triple Guaranteed

When you buy your Dinnerware at Wards—you are protected by Wards Triple Guarantee!

1—Wards guarantee Open Stock on all dinnerware, and we will obtain replacements as long as pattern is made by the pottery.

2—Wards guarantee prices 20 to 35% lower than most prices on comparable dinnerware.

3—Wards guarantee safe delivery—and complete satisfaction.

AND—Wards offer a NEW service—make up your own set—include just the pieces you want at an additional saving—See Page 319.

$2.49 20-Pc. · Colorful Gay Caliente Ware · $4.49 32-Pc.
NOW FULLY OVEN-PROOF

Caliente—so popular for informal dining—so gay and colorful for Spring and Summer meals! Wards prices are 20% to 30% less than elsewhere. *Approved by Good Housekeeping as oven-proof.* Comes in Tangerine, Yellow, Blue or Green. Put a complete service of one color at each place—or mix up the colors. First quality Triple-Selected American Semi-Porcelain. Colors are applied in the glaze—they can't wear off. See Page 319 for composition of sets.

When ordering Open Stock and Extra Pieces—Be sure to State Color: Tangerine, Blue, Yellow or Green.

486 B 6169—20-Piece Service for 4. One service of each color for 4 persons. Shipping weight 14 pounds **$2.49**

486 B 6171—32-Piece Service for 6. 2 Blue, 2 Yellow, 1 Tangerine, 1 Green Service, Green Vegetable Bowl, Yellow Platter. Shipping weight 23 pounds **$4.49**

(G) 586 B 6175—Creamer and Sugar. *State color.* Shipping weight 3 pounds **$1.18**

486 B 6172—53-Piece Service for 8. Two services of each color; Blue Sugar and Creamer, Green Vegetable Bowl and Yellow Platter. Shipping weight 42 pounds **$8.98**

586 B 6175—Open Stock. *State pattern, articles wanted and color*; Tangerine, Yellow, Blue or Green. See Page 319.

Matching Tumblers with Safe-Edge Rim

586 B 6645—9½-oz. Wt. 5 lbs. Set of 8 .....39c
586 B 6598—5-oz. Wt. 3 lbs. Set of 8 .....37c

586 B 6175—**Extra Pieces**. *State article and color*: Tangerine, Yellow, Blue or Green. Shipping weights: 2 lbs., 1 lb., 3 lbs., 8 oz., 2 lbs.
(B) Salt and Pepper Shakers..............43c
(E) Candlesticks. Pair 79c
(F) Ice Lip Jug, 64-oz 89c
(H) 6-(5-oz.) cup Teapot $1.29

Matching Oven-Proof Cooking Ware

(A) 586 B 6943 — Casserole with 7-in. pie plate cover. 1½-qt. capacity. Ship. wt. 5 lbs. *State Tangerine, Blue, Green or Yellow* ..95c

(C) 586 B 6940 — Modern 1½-Qt. Casserole. Yellow only. Chromium plated base. Black Bakelite handles. Shipping weight 7 lbs. **$1.59**

(D) 586 B 6942 — Large 10-in. Salad Bowl. Shipping weight 4 pounds. *State color*: Tangerine, Blue, Green or Yellow **$1.19**

586 B 6945—3-Piece Bowl Set (not shown). 7½-in.—Tangerine; 8¼-in.—Yellow; and 9¾-in.—Green. Shipping weight 5 pounds.....98c

Our Finest Casserole
Colorful Modern! Ovenproof Semi-Porcelain Casserole (7½-in. diam. holds about 2 qts.). Bake in the oven—serve on the table in the detachable Chromium-plated frame. Wt. ea. 5 lbs.
586 C 7682—Red Casserole, Yellow cover, Brown bakelite handles on frame. **$1.89**
586 C 7683—Blue Casserole, Yellow cover, White handles on frame......**$1.89**

NEW! CALIENTE RAINBOW
Dinner Set in Mixed Colors

$3.79 22-Pc. Set

A new idea for informal dining! In the 22-pc. set (service for 4) there is a complete set of one solid color service for each person—Tangerine, Yellow, Blue and Green. Put a complete outfit in front of each person, or mix up the colors—put the blue cup on tangerine, yellow or green saucer, put the yellow bread and butter plate with blue dinner plate, etc. The 32-pc. set (service for 6) includes 2 blue outfits, 2 yellow outfits, one tangerine outfit, one green outfit. 53-pc. set includes 2 outfits of each color. With all sets, vegetable bowl is green, platter, yellow. First Quality American Semi-Porcelain. *Mailable.*

486 A 6173—22-Pc. Set. Ship. wt. 18 lbs. .**$3.79**
586 A 6175—Creamer, Sugar. Ship. wt. 4 lbs. **1.00**
486 A 6171—32-Pc. Set. Ship. wt. 23 lbs. .. **4.79**
486 A 6172—53-Pc. Set. Ship. wt. 42 lbs. .. **9.98**
586 A 6175—Open Stock on Next Page. When ordering from open stock be sure to state colors wanted . . . *Tangerine, Yellow, Blue or Green.*

Reprints from 1930s and 1940s catalogs.

Caliente

Row 1: Tangerine sugar and cover, $22.00; cobalt blue shaker, $10.00; yellow teapot and cover, $45.00; cobalt 6" fruit plate, $10.00; Tangerine creamer, $12.00.

Row 2: Gray dinner plate, $20.00; turquoise bowl, $15.00; pink dinner plate, $20.00.

Row 3: Tangerine cream soup, $15.00; covered casserole, $30.00; turquoise candleholder, $12.00; turquoise cup/saucer set, $12.00.

All from the collection of John Moses.

Marks found on Paden City Pottery's ware. You will find other marks. Shell-Krest is also found as Shell-Crest. I believe this Papoco mark to be a Paden City mark but I have not been able to verify this information.

Advertisement for Paden City's Patio.

Row 1: Patio decoration on Shell-Krest shape platter, $20.00 – 25.00; Patio decoration oval vegetable bowl, $18.00 – 22.00.

Row 2: Patio decoration on 10" Shell-Krest shape plate, $10.00 – 15.00; Patio decoration fruit/sauce bowl, $6.00 – 8.00; Patio decoration on 10" Shell-Krest shape plate, $10.00 – 15.00.

Row 3: Nasturtium decoration on Shell-Krest shape covered sugar/creamer, $12.00 – 15.00; Nasturtium creamer, $10.00 – 12.00; Far East decoration on Shell-Krest plate, $8.00 – 10.00; Vermillion Rose decoration Shell-Krest shape shaker, $10.00 – 12.00; Nasturtium decoration gravy/sauce boat, $15.00 – 20.00.

Page 221

First two rows are Shenandoah ware.

Row 1: Strawberry 8" plate, $6.00 – 8.00; Jonquil 9" plate, $6.00 – 8.00; Poppy 7" plate, $6.00 – 8.00.

Row 2: All Morning Glory decoration sugar and cover, $15.00 – 18.00; creamer, $12.00 – 15.00; teapot, $35.00 – 40.00; Morning Glory 7" plate, $6.00 – 8.00.

Row 3: Floral covered casserole, $20.00 – 25.00; Vermillion Rose bowl, $15.00 – 18.00; Patio decoration covered casserole, $25.00 – 30.00.

Row 4: Bluebell 6" plate, $4.00 – 6.00; Floral fruit/sauce dish, $2.00 – 4.00; Red Rose decoration 6" plate, $4.00 – 6.00; Red Rose 6" plate, $4.00 – 6.00.

1940s ad for Paden City tableware.

Page 223

Row 1: Modern Orchid 6" plate, $6.00 – 8.00; Modern Orchid bowl, $6.00 – 8.00; fruit/sauce bowl, $4.00 – 6.00.

Row 2: Yellow Rose on Minion shape, introduced in 1952. 9" plate, $10.00 – 12.00; 7" plate, $6.00 – 8.00; cup/saucer, $8.00 – 12.00 set; creamer, $12.00 – 15.00; sugar and cover, $15.00 – 18.00.

Row 3: Duchess decoration on Tu-Tone shoulder 10" plate, $8.00 – 10.00; square luncheon plate, $8.00 – 10.00; English Ivy decoration saucer, $2.00 – 3.00; English Ivy decoration 7" plate, $6.00 – 8.00.

Row 4: Rose platter, $20.00 – 25.00; 7" plate, $6.00 – 8.00; 6" plate, $6.00 – 8.00; cup and saucer, $10.00 – 14.00 set.

Paden Bak-Serv Autumn Leaf.

Page 225

Row 1: Jonquil decoration sugar (lid missing), $10.00 – 12.00; Jonquil decoration creamer, $12.00 – 15.00; Posies cup/saucer, $10.00 – 14.00 set; Posies 6" plate, $4.00 – 6.00.

Row 2: Grandiose decoration meat platter, $20.00 – 25.00; Posies 6" plate, $4.00 – 6.00; 10" dinner plate, $8.00 – 10.00.

Row 3: Wild Rose on Princess 9" plate, $8.00 – 10.00; Wild Rose on Princess 7" plate, $6.00 – 8.00; Wild Rose individual baker, $8.00 – 10.00; teapot, $30.00 – 35.00; (These two pieces are marked Northern Products, Chicago, and may not be Paden City.)

Row 4: Shenandoah Ware in Farberware frame, $25.00 – 30.00; Corn is Green decoration designed by Anton Refergier, $20.00 – 25.00. (Other patterns designed by Anton Refergier for Paden City Pottery were Arabian Night, Design 44, The Rite of Spring, and Sea Shell.)

Page 227

Row 1: All Shell-Krest shape. Far East decoration creamer, $10.00 – 12.00; sugar and cover, $15.00 – 18.00; Acacia Flower creamer, $10.00 – 12.00; sugar and cover, $14.00 – 18.00.

Row 2: All Shell-Krest shape. Far East 9" plate, $10.00 – 12.00; fruit/sauce bowl, $6.00 – 8.00; Blossoms platter, $20.00 – 24.00.

Row 3: All Shell-Krest shape. Nasturtium decoration 9" plate, $8.00 – 10.00; Sunflower 6" plate, $6.00 – 8.00; Patio bowl, $8.00 – 10.00.

Row 4: Rust Tulip decoration on Shell-Krest shape 9" plate, $8.00 – 10.00; Tulip 6" plate, $6.00 – 8.00; Tulip decoration with cobalt/gold trim service plate, $12.00 – 16.00.

Advertisement for Shenandoah ware.

Pfaltzgraff Pottery

The present-day Pfaltzgraff Pottery traces its original roots back to the early 1800s and, with its predecessor companies, is one of the oldest manufacturers of pottery in the United States. The Pfaltzgraff family has been continuously involved in the manufacture of stoneware and related products since that time. The current president is Louis J. Appell, Jr., whose mother is a direct descendant of the first member of the family to conduct pottery manufacturing in this country. Today's Pfaltzgraff company is the outgrowth of a number of small pottery-making plants, which over the last century and a half existed in several localities in York County, Pennsylvania.

The Pfaltzgraff name originated in the Pfaltz area of the German Rhineland where the picturesque castle bearing the family name still stands. This famous landmark, seen by thousands of tourists each year, is reflected in the company's castle trademark.

One of the main concerns of life in the new United States in the early 1800s was the preservation of food for use in winter. To answer this need, the early products of the Pfaltzgraff company were storage crocks of stoneware with gray salt glaze and blue decoration which were used for pickles, sauerkraut, apple, butter, and salted meat; jugs for vinegar, hard and soft cider, and molasses — all the good foods that added variety to the hearty fare of the German and Scotch-Irish settlers. Any of these early Pfaltzgraff crocks or jugs that have survived bring a high price at antique shows today.

Serving the needs of the community has always been one of the company's major goals. Like many contemporaries of early America, a Pfaltzgraff pottery was one of the community's most popular gathering spots, particularly during cold Pennsylvania winters. Because of its warmth, the pottery was the scene of dances and other events. Advertisements in local papers offered facilities for baking beans with slow-simmered cooking while the kiln was being heated up to the high temperature necessary for the proper firing of stoneware.

As technical and sociological changes in living came, one by one the early potter's main products fell into disuse. Glass jars with sealed lids were invented which introduced a whole new way of preserving food. An ice-making machine made refrigeration more widespread. Tin vessels which were lighter and more durable than stoneware were cheap and readily available. Changes in smoking habits led to the disappearance of clay pipes. Glass replaced stoneware patent medicine bottles. A new tariff bill brought American potters in competition with lower-paid European workers, and in the 1920s the Prohibition Amendment ended a good market in stoneware whiskey jugs.

Thus, to stay in business, potters had to change with the times. To supplement its dwindling household stoneware business, Pfaltzgraff for many years produced animal and poultry feeders. In the early days of this century red clay flowerpots also became an important product line. As these products too began to yield to competition from other materials, Pfaltzgraff designers turned increasingly in the 1940s and 1950s to other forms of household products and to giftwares. Brightly colored mixing bowls, custard cups, planters, cookie jars, ashtrays, and similar products became the staples of the line. These early examples of the company's current products found a ready market in gift and variety stores.

Soon an even stronger demand was triggered for new Pfaltzgraff dinnerware and serving pieces. These stoneware products were beautiful enough to be used for special occasions, yet functional and sturdy enough to be used every day. Over the past 25 years Pfaltzgraff has introduced four extremely successful dinnerware lines — Gourmet, Heritage, Yorktowne, and Village, all still available with a wide range of accessories. To complement these wares the company manufactures tin and copper, and decorates glassware from other manufacturers.

Pflatzgraff backstamps.

In recent years Pfaltzgraff has expanded dramatically to meet consumer demand. Additional manufacturing facilities have been built in York and in nearby Adams County, including the largest pottery constructed in the United States since World War II. While time and technology have changed, the original character of Pfaltzgraff products, the Pfaltzgraff reputation for high quality at a reasonable price has not changed. The company continues to produce useful and attractive products with the same integrity and pride that have been a Pfaltzgraff tradition since the early days of the nineteenth century.

Even though the Pfaltzgraff Pottery's history dates back to 1805, the company as we know it today is a relative newcomer to dinnerware, as Pfaltzgraff made its first dinnerware in 1940.

Yorktowne

Heritage

Village

Gourmet

Pope Gosser China Company

The Pope Gosser China Company was located in Coshocton, Ohio, a member of the ill-fated American Chinaware Corporation until its demise in 1932. Its early ware does not have the appearance of quality ware. Pope Gosser did make some lovely ware in the forties as evidenced by the Florence pattern (shown below). Pope Gosser also made Rose Point and later sold the molds to Steubenville. You will find Rose Point made by both companies. The Canonsburg Pottery eventually wound up with the Rose Point molds and it, too, marketed Rose Point.

Florence 9" plate, $8.00 – 10.00; 6" plate, $6.00 – 8.00; fruit/sauce bowl, $4.00 – 6.00; cup, $6.00 – 8.00.

Pope Gosser backstamps.

Pottery Guild

Pottery Guild marked pieces have, until recently, been one of the big mysteries of dinnerware research.

Pottery Guild was a sales organization formed in 1937 by Mr. J. Block, founder of The Block China Company. Pottery Guild was granted a certificate of incorporation, August 10, 1937, in New York County and was dissolved by proclamation, March 8, 1946. Mr. Jay Block has remembrances of his father buying Pottery Guild ware from The Cronin Company, Minerva, Ohio. Pottery Guild Hostess Ware pieces were widely distributed through wholesale houses and catalog stores.

Pottery Guild backstamp.

CALICO FRUIT OVENWARE—GUARANTEED OVEN-PROOF AND ACID-PROOF

Wards Will Replace Any Piece that Cracks or Crazes in Course of Baking

Every Piece guaranteed oven-proof and acid-proof. A new kind of Ovenware. Light-weight American Semi-Porcelain—as attractive as your china dinnerware—heat-proof to bake in—beautiful to serve in. Smart "Calico Fruit" design in rich Blue, Green, Orange and Red over dainty Ivory background. Bake, serve and store in the same pretty dishes—save time—save dishwashing.

3-Piece Bowl Set $1¹⁹
(J) Holds 1½, 2¼ and 4½ pints. 6, 7 and 9-in. diams. Large bowl not recommended or oven use. Ship. wt., set 9 lbs. 586 B 6877—Set......$1.19

Custard Cups 12¢ Each
(K) For custards, cupcakes, clover leaf rolls, muffins, etc. Cap. ea. 5 oz. 3½-in. diam. Heat-proof. Shipping weight each 12 oz.
586 B 6878—Six.......69c
Each....................12c

482 WARDS ᴋ

Pitchers in 3 Sizes 44¢ 16-oz.
Heat-proof pitchers—for cream, milk, iced and hot drinks, etc.
(L) 586 B 6888—45-oz. 5½ in. high. Ship. wt. 3 lbs....74c
(M) 586 B 6887—30-oz. 4⅝ in. high. Ship. wt. 2 lbs....59c
(N) 586 B 6886—16-oz. 3¾ in. high. Ship. wt. 1 lb. 4 oz.44c

Range Set 89¢
(P) Saves steps at the stove. Pair of salt and pepper shakers, 2⅝-in. tall. Covered jar for drippings, 5 in. by 4½ in. high. Heat-proof.
586 B 6880—Wt. 2 lbs. 4 oz.89c

11-Piece Set $2²⁹
$2.94 Value! Includes: Covered Casserole and Plate, 9-in. Pie Plate, Server and 6 Custard Cups described separately. Ship. wt. 18 lbs.
586 B 6891—11-Pc. Set..$2.29

Beverage Pitcher 98¢
(R) Large—holds 5 pints. New shape with ice lip for easy pouring. 6½ in. high.
586B6885—Wt. 3 lbs. 8 oz.98c

3-Way Casserole $1¹⁹
(S) 3-Way! Use the 8-inch 1½-qt. Casserole covered or open—use the pie plate cover separately. Matching 9-inch plate included. Ship. wt. 8 lbs.
586 B 6870—Complete...$1.19

3-Piece Salad Set 98¢
(T) Big salad bowl, 9-in. diam. by 2⅝ in. deep. Matching fork and spoon included. Wt. 4 lbs. 4 oz.
586 B 6875—3-Pc. Set.....98c

Cookie Jar $1¹⁹
$1.49 Value
(U) Big 7½-pt. size! Snug inset cover keeps cookies fresh. 8 in. high, 8-in. diam.—good size for baking beans too. Heat-proof. Shipping weight 5 pounds.
586 B 6881................$1.19

3-Piece Waffle Set $1⁹⁸
(V) 3½-pt. covered Batter pitcher, 6 in. high; 1-pint covered Syrup Pitcher, 5 in. high. 11¾ by 8¼-in. Tray with Red band.
586 B 6882—Shipping weight 11 pounds.................$1.98

Heat-Proof Pie Plates 32¢ 9-in.
(W) Deep even-heating Pie Plates. Bake, serve, store in them. Heat-proof. Matching server below.
586 B 6873—9 inches. Shipping weight 2 pounds, 12 ounces....32c
586 B 6874—9¾ inches. Shipping weight 3 pounds.........37c
586 B 6879—Pie Server.
Ship. wt. 12 oz.............21c

32¢ 9-in. Pie Plate

1939 Wards catalog reprint.

Page 233

Row 1: Calico Flower small covered jug, $18.00 – 20.00; Sombrero jug (no lid), $15.00 – 18.00.

Row 2: Holland shape jug, Tulips, $30.00 – 35.00; Apples jug (lid missing), $30.00 – 35.00; ball jug, Pear, $35.00 – 40.00.

Row 3: Calico Fruit covered cookie jar, $55.00 – 60.00; Calico Fruit pie baker, $25.00 – 30.00.

Row 4: Hostess ware 11" salad bowl, Peach decoration, $45.00 – 50.00; Calico Teapot decoration on lid of covered casserole, $40.00 – 45.00.

Pottery Guild backstamp.

HOSTESS OVENWARE

15 PIECES—HEAT AND COLD RESISTANT—STUNNING PATTERN IN 5 COLORS, PLATINUM STRIPES

- Handled Cake Plate (12 inch) and Server
- Ball Beverage Jug — 2½ quarts
- Holland Beverage Jug — 2½ quarts
- Salad Bowl — 11 inch
- Casserole with Pie Cover—1½ quarts
- Handled Pie Plate (10 inch) and Server
- Range Set (4 Pieces)

A new and beautiful set of genuine Pottery Guild, oven-proof Hostessware. It's the latest type of baking and tableware, a light-weight, oven-proof pottery that is as attractive as china dinnerware, yet is unconditionally guaranteed heat-proof. With this practical set you can prepare, bake, serve, and store—without changing dishes! That means fewer dishes to wash! You'll enjoy preparing foods in this handsome Hostessware. You can bake in it, then serve in it—even use it for storing in your refrigerator, for it is positively guaranteed against breakage from either heat or cold. The set of fifteen pieces pictured above is a beautiful ensemble of Ivory with a china-like finish. Each piece is decorated with a lovely Peach pattern that is a blend of brilliant, fade-proof colors. An outstanding value!
Shipping weight 50 lbs.
A70110 Complete Set...................... **$12.50**

Ad for Hostess Ovenware from trade publication.

Purinton Pottery

The Purinton Pottery was opened in 1936 in Wellsville, Ohio, by Bernard Purinton. Purinton continued to operate at that location until 1941 when the pottery was relocated to Shippenville, Pennsylvania. Ground-breaking for the Shippenville-Purinton plant was in 1941 and open house for the new 300'x100' plant was November 21, 1941. The first ware was drawn on Pearl Harbor Day, December 7, 1941. Officers were: president, Bernard S. Purinton; sales manager, J. M. Hammer; secretary/treasurer, William J. Bower. The Shippenville Chamber of Commerce was instrumental in Purinton's move to Shippenville.

The Purinton Pottery did only hand painting, using no decals. Purinton employed 100 workers from the area and provided an annual income of $140,000. William H. Blair and Dorothy Purinton were chief designers. Harry Blair Purinton tells us that the Apple pattern was the company's first and best pattern.

A newspaper account from *The Derrick* tells of the plant's closing on May 30, 1958. Plans were pending to bring in outside management and sales help to reorganize and reopen the plant. On further investigation, we determined that "outside help" to be the Taylor-Smith-Taylor Company of Chester, West Virginia.

Final closing of the Purinton Pottery of Shippenville, Pennsylvania, is believed to be 1959. The end of a 61-year pottery association for the family, dating back to 1898 when Bernard Purinton's father, John, helped form the United States Pottery Company of Wellsville, Ohio.

Purinton made a line of solid color shapes for Rubel, a New York sales organization. These pieces were marketed under the name of Rubel.

Purinton backstamps.

Apple Pattern

All hand-painted Purinton Apple decoration.

Page 235
Row 1: 12 oz. tumbler, $16.00 – 18.00; 6 oz. juice tumbler, $14.00 – 16.00; salt and pepper set, each piece, $10.00 – 12.00; cup/saucer set, $18.00 – 20.00.

Row 2: Sugar jar, $75.00 – 85.00; 7" plate, $8.00 – 10.00; cookie jar, $75.00 – 85.00.

Row 3: 2-pint jug, $35.00 – 40.00; drippings jar, $18.00 – 20.00; 1-pint jug, $20.00 – 25.00.

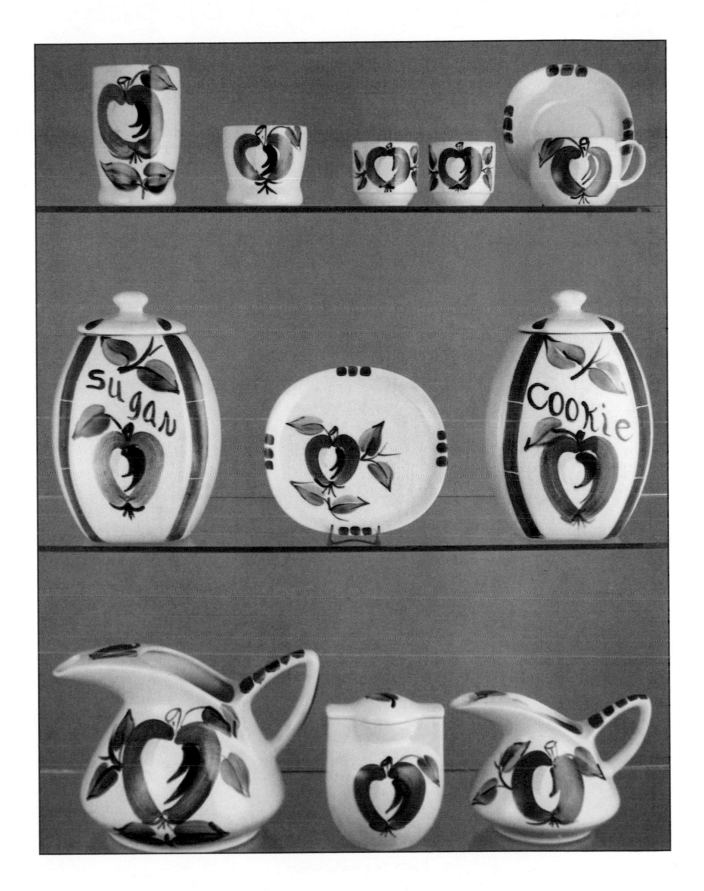

Red Wing Pottery Company

Red Wing Pottery Company was founded in Red Wing, Minnesota, in 1878. Red Wing produced crocks, stoneware, and jugs until changing times in the 1920s caused a lack of interest in these products. Red Wing changed its trend in the 1920s with a line of art pottery and more importantly added a colored dinnerware line, Gypsy Trail, in the 1930s.

Red Wing added a hand-painted dinnerware line in the 1940s and by the 1950s had captured the dinnerware market with its Bob White pattern. An Anniversary Group was introduced in 1953, the 75th anniversary of Red Wing. Capistrana and Country Gardens were patterns from the Anniversary Group. Both patterns were on Red Wing's Tweed Tex surface texture.

A strike hit the company June 1, 1967. Liquidation began in August 1967 and was completed in 1969. Red Wing dinnerware was sold at the pottery several years after the manufacturing was discontinued.

Turquoise Town and Country teapot, designed by Eva Zeisel in the 1940s for the Red Wing Pottery Company, $300.00 – 350.00.

 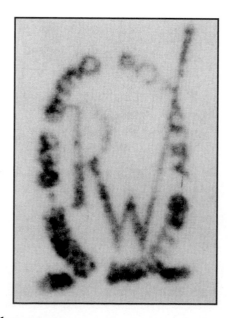

Red Wing backstamps.

Lexington Rose

Row 1: Teapot, $45.00 – 50.00; cup/saucer, $12.00 – 15.00 set; 10" plate, $10.00 – 12.00.

Row 2: Creamer, $15.00 – 20.00; sugar, $20.00 – 22.00; gravy/sauce boat, $20.00 – 22.00; liner, $12.00 – 15.00.

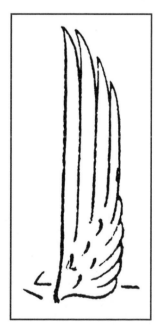

Red Wing backstamps.

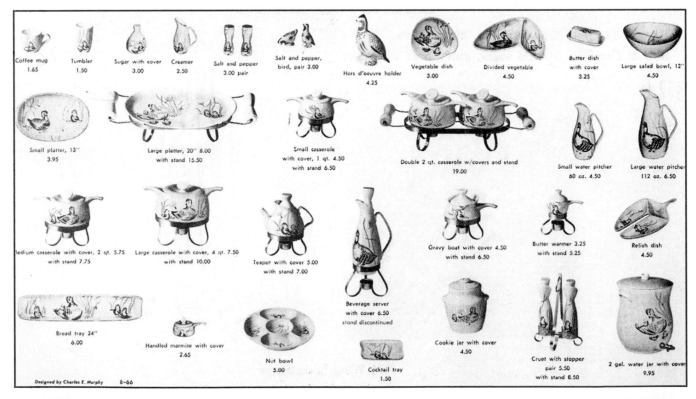

Red Wing's Bob White dinnerware has been declared by some as the most popular pattern of the 1950s. Bob White was designed by Charles Murphy who later went to work for the Stetson Company, Lincoln, Illinois.

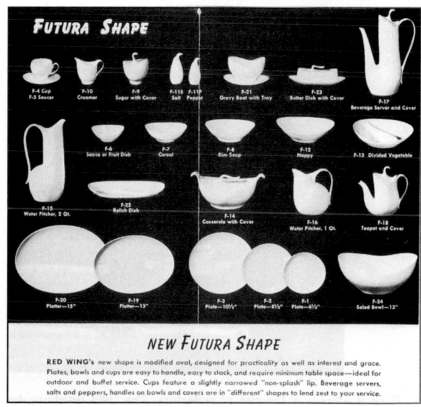

NEW FUTURA SHAPE

RED WING's new shape is modified oval, designed for practicality as well as interest and grace. Plates, bowls and cups are easy to handle, easy to stack, and require minimum table space—ideal for outdoor and buffet service. Cups feature a slightly narrowed "non-splash" lip. Beverage servers, salts and peppers, handles on bowls and covers are in "different" shapes to lend zest to your service.

Tampico on the Futura shape, 1950s.

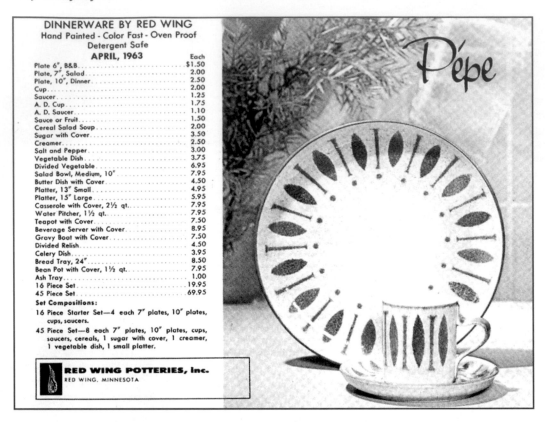

DINNERWARE BY RED WING
Hand Painted - Color Fast - Oven Proof
Detergent Safe

APRIL, 1963

	Each
Plate 6", B&B	$1.50
Plate, 7", Salad	2.00
Plate, 10", Dinner	2.50
Cup	2.00
Saucer	1.25
A. D. Cup	1.75
A. D. Saucer	1.10
Sauce or Fruit	1.50
Cereal Salad Soup	2.00
Sugar with Cover	3.50
Creamer	2.50
Salt and Pepper	3.00
Vegetable Dish	3.75
Divided Vegetable	6.95
Salad Bowl, Medium, 10"	7.95
Butter Dish with Cover	4.50
Platter, 13" Small	4.95
Platter, 15" Large	5.95
Casserole with Cover, 2½ qt.	7.95
Water Pitcher, 1½ qt.	7.95
Teapot with Cover	7.50
Beverage Server with Cover	8.95
Gravy Boat with Cover	7.50
Divided Relish	4.50
Celery Dish	3.95
Bread Tray, 24"	8.50
Bean Pot with Cover, 1½ qt.	7.95
Ash Tray	1.00
16 Piece Set	19.95
45 Piece Set	69.95

Set Compositions:

16 Piece Starter Set—4 each 7" plates, 10" plates, cups, saucers.

45 Piece Set—8 each 7" plates, 10" plates, cups, saucers, cereals, 1 sugar with cover, 1 creamer, 1 vegetable dish, 1 small platter.

RED WING POTTERIES, Inc.
RED WING, MINNESOTA

Pépe

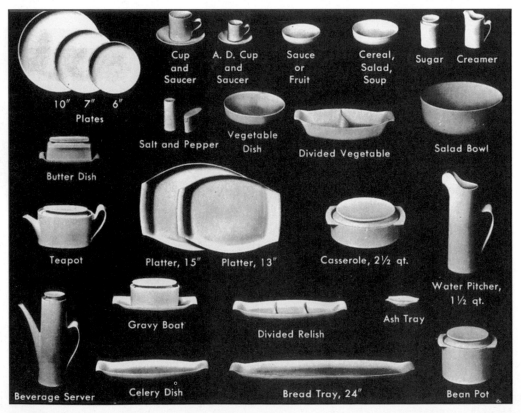

Pépe is already a favorite of collectors. The 1963 brochure describes Pépe as "a dramatic Spanish motif of the modern school." Flecked beige undertones are highlighted with sunbursts of bittersweet and deep mauve.

Village Green is another popular collectible Red Wing pattern. Heavy and substantial, Village Green is second in popularity only to Red Wing's Bob White. Mid-1950s.

Royal China Company

Royal China Company is located in Sebring, Ohio. The Royal China Company was formerly the old E. H. Sebring plant. Everyone that I have talked to credits the success of Royal to Beatrice Miller. The Royal plant expanded and eventually became part of the Jeannette operation. Royalton was Royal's trade name for its plastic dinnerware line.

Royal China backstamp.

Royal Currier & Ives 6" plate, $8.00 – 10.00; covered bowl, $25.00 – 28.00; 7" plate, $10.00 – 12.00; dinner plate, $14.00 – 16.00.

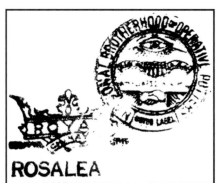

Royal China backstamps.

Royal Gold Lace salt & pepper set, $15.00 – 20.00; creamer, $15.00 – 18.00.

For GENUINE **ROYAL**
BLUE WILLOW underglaze
LOOK FOR THIS BACKSTAMP

BLUE WILLOW
by
Royal
SEBRING OHIO

- **The demand is terrific.**
- **Delivery at once from our stockpile.**
- **And also available is Pink and Green Willow.**

NEWSPAPER MATS FURNISHED

BLUE WILLOW
by
Royal
SEBRING OHIO

Please write for price lists today.

SEBRING, OHIO

8-Pc.
**BARBECUE
SERVING
SET**

unusual value at **4.95** *retail*

- For patio, buffet, barbecue or everyday use! Set serves 4 people!
- 4 large 10¼" plates; nest, stack and lock for easy handling!
- 4 non-tip 11-ounce mugs with large, easy-to-carry handles!
- Plates deeply partitioned so liquids won't merge!
- Lightweight; made of hard, durable earthenware, by Royal China!
- Gay sketchbook patterns printed UNDER the glaze!
- Patterns guaranteed not to wash off nor fade, even in dishwasher!
- For indoor or outdoor use! Perfect shower or hostess gift!

ROYAL CHINA, *Inc.*
Sebring, Ohio

Advertisements from the late 1940s and early 1950s for Royal China.

CAVALIER iron stone

Genuine American Ironstone by Royal China

Quality CAVALIER Ironstone is produced by skilled craftsmen in America's most modern pottery. With the addition of eight new patterns, Royal is more exciting, more sales appealing than ever.

BETTER STYLING . . . MORE VERSATILITY
Genuine American Ironstone by Royal China . . . seventeen distinctive patterns that make their statement quietly but effectively. Accentuated with today's fashion colors, Royal's superbly styled casual dinnerware is at home on a buffet table or at a formal dinner party. Royal . . . the most versatile, most desirable line of medium-priced dinnerware in the industry.

Brentwood

Triple Treat

Clear Day

Overture

Casablanca

Currier & Ives

A Royal China brochure.

A Royal China brochure.

Salem China Company

Biddam Smith, John McNichol, and Dan Cronin are credited with the founding of the Salem China Company in 1898 in Salem, Ohio. They had been with the Standard Pottery operation in East Liverpool, Ohio. They had been pessimistic about the future of the pottery growth in East Liverpool. There was little activity in the new operation and by 1918 the business needed a considerable amount of capital to continue.

F. A. Sebring was given an option on the Salem plant in 1918. F. A. was looking for a spot for his son returning from the war. Floyd McKee was asked to rejoin the Sebrings and to manage the Salem operation until Frank Jr. (Tode) was discharged.

Possession was taken in August 1918. McKee retired in 1950 and became chairman of the board. At that time J. Harrison Keller became president and general manager. The Salem China Company stopped manufacturing in 1967. Ware was made out of the country for several years.

A variety of marks was used on Salem pieces over the years, some of which are shown here.

Salem China Company backstamps.

Row 1: 6" Basket plate, $4.00 – 5.00; 8" Basket plate, $6.00 – 8.00; Colonial ashtray in Farberware frame, $18.00 – 25.00.

Row 2: Yellowridge 9" plate, $12.00 – 14.00; 6" plate, Bluebird decoration, $15.00 – 20.00; 9" Maple Leaf plate, $8.00 – 10.00.

Row 3: Goldtrim 6" plate, $4.00 – 6.00; Goldtrim butter pat, $4.00 – 6.00; June decoration on 7" Briar Rose shape plate, $6.00 – 8.00; June decoration on 9" Briar Rose shape plate, $8.00 – 10.00.

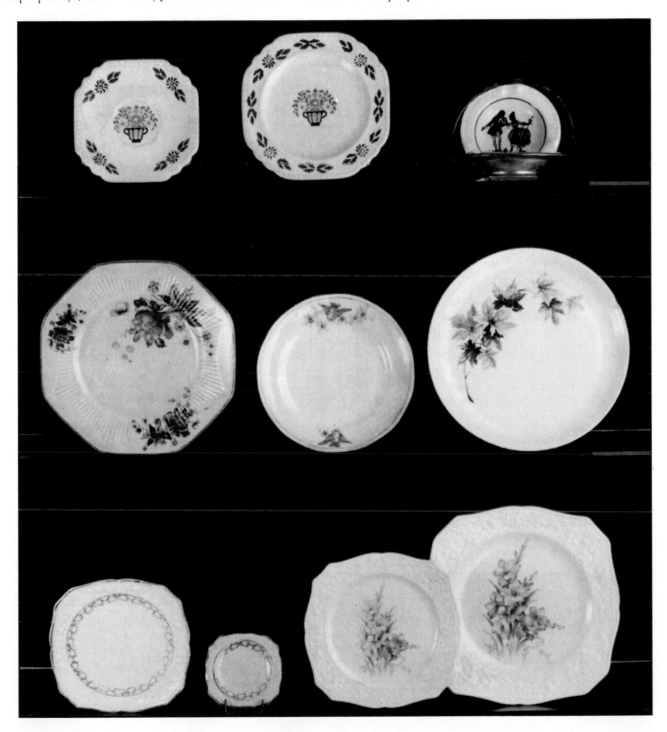

Page 249
Row 1: Tulip decoration on Streamline shape covered sugar, $18.00 – 20.00; creamer, $15.00 – 18.00; cup/saucer set, $12.00 – 15.00 set; Sailing on Tricome shape, $12.00 – 15.00.

Row 2: Mandarin Red on Streamline shape sugar and cover, $30.00 – 35.00; creamer, $25.00 – 30.00; cup, $15.00 – 18.00; Sailing plate on Tricome shape, $15.00 – 18.00.

Row 3: Rust Tulip decoration on Victory shape platter, $18.00 – 20.00; Rust Tulip 6" plate, $4.00 – 6.00; 8" plate, $6.00 – 8.00; square plate, $6.00 – 8.00.

Row 4: Petit Point Basket 9" plate, $8.00 – 10.00; shaker, $8.00 – 10.00; 7" plate, $6.00 – 8.00; Bryn-Mawr decoration on Symphony shape, $8.00 – 10.00.

Salem backstamps.

SALEM CHINAWARE FOR QUALITY and LASTING BEAUTY

Carolyn Service Plates

They add that extra touch of color and decoration to any table setting. Striking floral design with heavy embellished border accent their beauty. Colored rims are overlaid with a beautiful filigree of 23K. gold. Wide gold line adorns the edge. Center design shows full blown rose in a nest of blue and green leaves, surrounded by dainty pink and yellow flower. **Carolyn Service Plates** are available in a choice of colored rims: Maroon, Pink, Blue or Green. **State color rim desired.** Packed 6 of a color to a carton.

Shipping weight, 11 pounds.
1290E585. Per set of 6..............**$9.50**

Godey Prints Service Plates

Nothing could be lovelier than this modern dinner table setting, based on the old-time themes of Grandmother's day, of vivid colors and lavender and lace. Three different Godey Prints are featured throughout the Service Plate set, each authentically reproduced in warmth of color, quaintness of style and clearness of detail. Wide heavy border comes in maroon, pink, blue or green with delicate gold filigree over the color and shoulder of the plate. The edge is banded in 23-kt. gold. Truly a delightful pattern for anyone who cherishes the beauty and loveliness of things old fashioned, brought down to us from days gone by. Packed 6 of color to carton. Shipping weight, 11 pounds.

State color rim desired.
1289E625. Per set of 6..............**$10.00**

Features of Salem China.—American china (semi-porcelain) body. Flawless, permanent, underglaze decoration. Patented process develops light weight. Bodies are exceptionally non-brittle. Shapes developed by famous stylists. Open stock.

COMPOSITION OF SALEM SETS

35-Piece Set	53-Piece Set
(Ship. wgt. 25 lbs.)	(Ship. wgt. 38 lbs.)
6—Cups	8—Cups
6—Saucers	8—Saucers
6—Dinner Plates 9 in.	8—Dinner Plates 9 in.
6—B & B Plates 6 in.	8—B & B Plates 6 in.
6—Fruits	8—Coupe Soups 7 in.
1—Meat Platter 11 in.	8—Fruits
1—Open Veg. Dish 8 in.	1—Cov. Sugar (2 Pcs.)
1—Cov. Sugar Bowl (2 Pcs.)	1—Cream Pitcher
1—Cream Pitcher	1—Meat Platter 11 in.
	1—Open Veg. Dish 8 in.

100-Piece Set	
(Shipping weight, 80 lbs.)	
12—Cups	1—Open Veg. Dish 8 in.
12—Saucers	1—Gravy Bowl 1 pt.
12—Dinner Plates 9 in.	1—Meat Platter 11 in.
12—Pie Plates 7 in.	1—Meat Platter 13 in.
12—B & B Plates 6 in.	1—Cream Pitcher
12—Coupe Soups 7 in.	1—Cov. Sugar (2 Pcs.)
12—Fruit Dishes	1—Cov. Veg. Dish (2-Pc.)
6—Oatmeals	
1—Open Butter Dish	

Commodore Pattern

Always in good taste and harmonizes with any table setting. 23K. gold of unusual beauty and appeal. Delicately traced border and classic medallions of gold.

Nation wide acceptance among all types of stores and buyers has proven the continued popularity for this type of pattern. Featured on the plain Symphony Shape with wide rims and creamy white surface, making a perfect background for a pattern of this kind.

1286E965. 35-Pc. set	**$17.50**
1287E1395. 53-Pc. set	**$26.00**
1288E2650. 100-Pc. set	**$50.00**

BRYN-MAWR PATTERN

Gay, charming floral sprays in soft, dual-tone colors of brown, lavender and gray with an edge line of platinum gold on an ivory white translucent semi-porcelain body. New, gracefully shaped handles and feet add that extra appearance that brings forth praise. You get years of pleasure and service from every piece.

8676E975. 35-Pc. Set...**$18.50**	8677E1450. 53-Pc. Set...**$28.50**	8679E2750. 100-Pc. Set...**$55.00**

INDIAN TREE

Originally created by the celebrated English designer, Thomas Minton, in the 18th Century, this design has been popular ever since. This pattern gives you a combination of a beautiful legend, plus a lovely decoration. This pattern is rich in gay flowers, featuring deep pinks, blues, and yellows supported by colorful foliage. It has real eye-appeal and is meeting with splendid acceptance on the part of discriminating buyers.

7537E825. 35-Pc. Set....**$16.50**	7538E1225. 53-Pc. Set....**$24.50**	7540E2650. 100-Pc. Set....**$52.50**

ROHDE-SPENCER CO., CHICAGO (6) ILL.—61

Salem advertisement from 1940s wholesale catalog.

Dinner Sets

"Basket of Tulips"

EX5041— 32 Pc. Set _ _ _ $10.90
EX5042— 53 Pc. Set _ _ _ 21.40
EX5043—100 Pc. Set _ _ _ 41.20

The various colored Spring Tulips on our Bonjour shape makes this a friendly pleasing pattern; finished with a wide Platinum band. This set reflects quaint charm and dignity.

"Standard"

EX5044— 32 Pc. Set _ _ _ $12.60
EX5045— 53 Pc. Set _ _ _ 24.60
EX5046—100 Pc. Set _ _ _ 47.50

For those who do not want an extreme modernistic shape — the white beauty of the ware and the four narrow floral sprays of buds combined, make this an attractive and desirable number. Its beauty is enhanced by a blue edge line.

"Tulip"

EX5047— 32 Pc. Set _ _ _ $9.80
EX5048— 53 Pc. Set _ _ _ 19.20
EX5049—100 Pc. Set _ _ _ 37.00

The most outstanding feature of this pattern is the vividly blended colors of the Tulip. The decorations set on the side of the plate is most unusual and attractive.

"Formal"

EX5050— 32 Pc. Set _ _ _ $13.10
EX5051— 53 Pc. Set _ _ _ 25.70
EX5052—100 Pc. Set _ _ _ 49.60

Colors which are a "natural!" This pattern is decorated with a ¼" Rust and Gold outer border, and a 1", 22 carat Gold design on the inside border. Any hostess will appreciate the pleasing variation this pattern offers.

"Cadet Series"

EX5053— 32 Pc. Set _ _ _ $12.60
EX5054— 53 Pc. Set _ _ _ 24.60
EX5055—100 Pc. Set _ _ _ 47.50

Sophistication is predominant. This set will make a smart inviting dinner table. It is a delightful expression of modern decoration.

COMPOSITION OF SETS (For composition of smaller sets see opposite page)

100 Pc. Set *(Shipping Weight 80 lbs.)*

Popular Sized Sets				Cambridge Crystal Glassware Pages 226 and 227
12 Cups	12 Coupe Soups 7"	1 Gravy Boat	1 Covd. Sugar (2 Pcs.)	
12 Saucers	12 Fruits	1 Cheese Plate	1 Covd. Veg. Dish (2 Pcs.)	
12 Dinner Plates 9"	1 Ob. Open Veg. Dish 9"	1 Meat Platter 11"	1 Jelly Bowl	
12 B and B Plates 6"	1 Rd. Open Veg. Dish 8"	1 Meat Platter 13"	1 Covd. Butter (3 Pcs.)	
12 Pie Plates 7"	1 Pickle Dish	1 Cream Pitcher		

Salem advertisement from 1940s wholesale catalog.

Dinnerware

List Prices Subject to Catalog Discount

•• COLORFUL, new and smart patterns styled to thrill the modern housewife.

"Dutch Petit Point"

EX5019—32 Pc. Set ... $ 9.90
EX5020—53 Pc. Set ... 19.40
EX5021—100 Pc. Set ... 37.50

Very colorful is this Petit Point design of a Dutch Boy and Girl, worked in red, blue and warm light brown on a cream background and red and blue bands on the border. An interpretation of an authentic Dutch masterpiece, done in Petit Point needlework design. Bonjour shape.

For Composition

of Sets

See PP. 224-225

"Sailing"

EX5018½—32 Pc. Set _ _ _ _ _ _ _ $10.40
EX5018—53 Pc. Set _ _ _ _ _ _ _ 20.40

Unusually smart, this streamlined design is a reproduction of a well-known artist's version of a ship motif. The coral and black sailboats with their guiding stars are reminiscent of the bright sails of an old-world fishing fleet. Set off by coral and platinum lined edges.

"Summer Day"

EX5022—32 Pc. Set—$10.40
EX5023—53 Pc. Set— 20.40
EX5024—100 Pc. Set— 39.40

Lovely harmony of color and balance are reflected in this pattern of a smart blue and white flower pot, in which sprays of red, black and green flowers are artistically placed. The Bonjour shape is lovely to look at and practical to use.

All Priced

F. O. B. New York

or Factory at Salem, Ohio.

New 24-PIECE CUP-PLATE **BRIDGE SET**
With Beverage Glasses to Match

Mandarin   Tricorne

"Monogram"

EX5015— 35 Pc. Set _ _ _ _ _ _ _ _ _ _ _ _ _ _ _ $14.90
EX5016— 53 Pc. Set _ _ _ _ _ _ _ _ _ _ _ _ _ _ _ 23.10
EX5017—100 Pc. Set _ _ _ _ _ _ _ _ _ _ _ _ _ _ _ 48.10

The essence of "smartness" is reflected in a dinner table set with monogrammed silver, glassware and dishes. This lovely streamlined pattern is beautifully decorated in 23 karat gold; available with any desired initial. (Monogrammed Dinnerware is made to order and requires a few extra days for shipping.)

Salem advertisements from 1940s wholesale catalog.

**Prices Subject to Catalog Discount
See Page 1A**

"Rose-Marie"

EX5026—	32 Pc. Set	$12.60
EX5027—	53 Pc. Set	24.60
EX5028—	100 Pc. Set	47.50

The entire center of the plate is covered by a cluster of Rose Buds of various soft pastels. A touch of Platinum on the edge produces a stimulating effect and adds a note of elegance.

"Aristocrat"

EX5029—	32 Pc. Set	$16.40
EX5030—	53 Pc. Set	32.10
EX5031—	100 Pc. Set	62.10

The established popular Century Shape with a smart new decoration. The entire border is finished in Delphinium Blue with four narrow black lines superimposed on the inner edge. Bordering this is an inner Platinum band. The hollow ware of this set is allover Delphinium Blue with black lines and Platinum bands and white interiors.

"Fruit Basket"

EX5032—	32 Pc. Set	$12.60
EX5033—	53 Pc. Set	24.60
EX5034—	100 Pc. Set	47.50

A distinctive pattern in both shape and decoration. Delightful little Fruit Baskets form the border of rich colors. All offset by an unusual narrow Checkerboard band in black and yellow on the edge. This dinner set will look well on any table and will reflect the good taste of the hostess.

"Jeanette"

EX5035—	32 Pc. Set	$9.80
EX5036—	53 Pc. Set	19.20
EX5037—	100 Pc. Set	37.00

A somewhat conventional pattern on our New Yorker Shape—the lightly embossed edge and the tinted ware blend beautifully with the new flower pot decoration. The colors are a harmonious blend of soft blues, yellows and orange.

"Victory"

EX5038—	32 Pc. Set	$8.70
EX5039—	53 Pc. Set	17.00
EX5040—	100 Pc. Set	32.80

The graceful lines and perfect symmetry that characterizes this handsome set make it unusually smart and popular. The border deviates from the standard floral embossing by being fluted. The handles on the hollow pieces are convenient and attractive. Although undecorated, this pattern has a stateliness hard to surpass.

COMPOSITION OF SETS (For composition of larger set see opposite page)

Composition of 53 Pc. Set

6 Cups	6 Fruits
6 Saucers	1 Meat Platter
6 Dinner Plates 9"	1 Open Vegetable Dish
6 B & B Plates 6"	

(Shipping Weight about 22 lbs.)

Guaranteed Safe Delivery

Composition of 32 Pc. Set

8 Cups	8 Fruits
8 Saucers	1 Vegetable Dish 8"
8 Dinner Plates 10"	1 Meat Platter 13"
8 B & B Plates 6"	1 Creamer
8 Coupe Soups 7"	1 Covd. Sugar Bowl (2 Pcs.)

(Shipping Weight about 39 lbs.)

Salem China advertisement from 1940s catalog.

MODERN DINNERWARE
Introducing the New VICTORY SHAPE
with decorations to enhance its natural beauty.

DINNER SETS SHOWN ON THIS PAGE ARE MADE UP OF THE FOLLOWING PIECES

32-Pc. Set:	53-Pc. Set:	100-Pc. Set	
6—Cups	8—Dinner Plates 9″	12—Cups	1—Meat Platter 11″
6—Saucers	8—Bread & Butter Plates 6″	12—Saucers	1—Meat Platter 13″
6—Dinner Plates 9″	8—Coupe Soups 6″	12—Dinner Plates 9″	1—Jelly Bowl
6—Bread & Butter Plates 6″	8—Fruits	12—Pie Plates 7″	1—Cov. Butter (3-pcs.)
6—Fruits	8—Cups	12—B & B Plates 6″	1—Cheese Plate 6″
1—Meat Platter 11″	8—Saucers	12—Coupe Soups 6″	1—Gravy Boat
1—Open Vegetable Dish 8″	1—Covered Sugar (2-pcs.)	12—Fruits	1—Cov. Sugar (2-pcs.)
	1—Creamer	1—Ob. Open Veg. Dish 9″	1—Cream Pitcher
	1—Platter 11″	1—Rd. Open Veg. Dish 8″	1—Covd. Veg. Dish (2-pcs.)
	1—Open Vegetable Dish 8″	1—Pickle Dish	

Doily Petit Point

This "Doily Petit Point" pattern on the new Victory shape is an outstanding contribution to modern designing. This very beautiful pattern embodies all the dignity and grace of rare old lace. The design features a beautiful rose center with a floral border, all worked out in the new Petit Point or cross-stitch design. The handles are all treated with a wide gold bar giving added attractiveness to this decoration. A fawn background adds the final touch to this lovely pattern.

The shape is the new "Victory," designed by a noted ceramic designer of the Cleveland Art School. Surely if you are interested in fine furnishings for that home of yours this beautifully shaped chinaware so smartly decorated will appeal to you. You will find listed below three different size sets, one to meet the requirements of any size family.

NO. 22K10
32 PC. SET
$9.25

NO. 22K11
53 PC. SET
$15.70

NO. 22K12
100 PC. SET
$32.00

"Jane Adams" Pattern

Bright gay flowers feature this decoration, with yellows and greens predominating. Dainty orchid buds also enhance the attractiveness of this lovely design. It is a two spray design. The handles are treated in appropriate colors.

This "Jane Adams" pattern is as attractive as a refreshing summer floral spray. It sets off the modern dining table to such great advantage that knowing hostesses are unusually enthusiastic about it. You, too, can be sure that what it does for other tables it most assuredly can do for yours. The new "Victory" shape forms a perfect background for the smartness of its modern pattern. You will be interested in knowing that this shape was designed by a noted ceramic designer of the Cleveland Art School. This is truly a lovely shape.

NO. 22K13
32 PC. SET
$9.25

NO. 22K14
53 PC. SET
$15.70

NO. 22K15
100 PC. SET
$32.00

**A SMART, MODERN SHAPE SET OFF BY
ATTRACTIVE DESIGNING**

Salem China advertisement from 1940s catalog.

Salem China Co.
Box 277, Salem, Ohio

Salem backstamps.

Scio Pottery Company

The Scio Pottery Company was founded by Lew Reese in 1932. The plant had been built in Scio in 1920 as an additional production plant by Albright of Carrollton, Ohio. The operation was closed in 1927.

Lew Reese visited Scio in 1932 and looked over the abandoned plant. The property was purchased by Reese at a sheriff's sale for $8,000.00 on a time payment plan. He immediately started living in a corner of the plant and making repairs on it.

By February 1933 the Scio-Ohio Pottery Company lacked funds for a payroll, raw materials, and orders. The story goes that a clay salesman got his company to advance clay and Reese himself went to Chicago and persuaded a large firm to take the first carload of cups. When the first payroll fell due, Lew Reese had a cash balance of 11 cents. Twenty townspeople put up $100.00 a piece and Scio began a history that has spanned nearly a half-century.

Row 1, top: Creamer, $25.00 – 28.00.

Row 2, middle: 7" plate, $10.00 – 12.00; sugar and cover, $30.00 – 35.00; cup/saucer set, $12.00 – 15.00.

Row 3, front: 9" plate, $12.00 – 15.00.

All Scio's Ranson shape with Hazel decoration.

All Currier & Ives.

Row 1: Creamer, $25.00 – 28.00; sugar and cover, $30.00 – 35.00.

Row 2: Fruit/sauce bowl, $6.00 – 8.00; cup/saucer set, $12.00 – 15.00.

Row 3: 10" plate, $12.00 – 15.00.

All Dorset decoration.

Row 1: Sugar and cover, $30.00 – 35.00; creamer, $25.00 – 28.00.

Row 2: Fruit/sauce bowl, $6.00 – 8.00; cup/saucer set, $12.00 – 15.00.

Row 3: 10" plate, $12.00 – 15.00.

Sebring Potteries

George A. Sebring had five sons: Oliver, George E., Ellsworth H., Frank A., and Joseph Sebring. The father had worked in the potteries and seemed to be content doing just that.

In 1887 in East Liverpool, Ohio, a pottery was formed by George Ashbaugh, Samson Turnbull, and the Sebring Brothers. Frank A. soon became the leader of the brothers.

The Sebring Brothers,* Ashbaugh and Turnbull, were able to take over the Agner Fautts Pottery for $12,500.00. They all did what was necessary and reopened the plant with $7,000.00. Soon after the plant was opened, Ashbaugh and Turnbull pulled out, the Sebrings buying their share for $11,000.00.

The Sebrings leased the East Palestine pottery plant in 1893. They were offered a bonus to build a plant in East Palestine (Ohio China Co.). In 1899, the Sebrings bought a large plot of land in Mahoning County, Ohio, just four miles from Alliance. They sold their interest and concentrated on Sebring, Ohio, and some of their plants included Sebring, Oliver, French China, and Limoges China. Around the 1920s or late-teens, the Sebrings purchased the Salem China Works.

The Sebrings are a study within themselves. They were involved with many potteries and change of names of potteries over the years. They also founded Sebring, Florida, but it was not a pottery location.

Sebring backstamps.

Page 259 – All Sebring's Heirloom shape, Corinthian decoration.
Row 1: Cup/saucer set, $10.00 – 12.00; fruit/sauce dish, $2.00 – 4.00; 7" plate, $4.00 – 6.00.

Row 2: 9" plate, $10.00 – 12.00; covered vegetable bowl, $35.00 – 40.00.

Row 3: Teapot, $40.00 – 50.00; gravy/sauce boat, $15.00 – 20.00; 8" plate, $6.00 – 8.00.

Row 4: Platters, $25.00 – 28.00 each.

* One source credits Ashbaugh and Turnbull as early Sebring partners and yet another source reports the early partners to be S. J. Cripps and Ashbaugh. Rarely will you find positive information concerning the early history of the pottery people.

Shawnee Pottery

A chance finding of an Indian arrowhead by Malcolm Schweiker created the interest to research what tribes had lived along the Muskingum. Mr. Schweiker discovered that Shawnee settlements had once been in the area and he named his new pottery "Shawnee."

The new Shawnee Pottery was housed in the former American Encaustic Tiling Company in Zanesville, Ohio. The date was 1937. Addis E. Hull, Jr., resigned from the A. E. Hull Pottery of Crooksville to manage the newly-formed Shawnee Pottery.

Hostilities toward other countries were beginning to build in the late 1930s and buyers were looking for American-made ware. Shawnee was able to get several accounts and, in 1938, George Rum Rill of Rum Rill Pottery suggested working with Shawnee. Rum Rill was not a manufacturer but a jobber or sales organization.

Many changes took place during the war years but operation resumed in 1946. Malcolm Schweiker sold his interest and Addis Hull resigned. By 1954, like many American potteries, Shawnee was suffering from an operating loss. Also in 1954, John Bonistall came to Shawnee to serve as vice-president and general manager.

Bonistall is credited with breathing new life into the dying pottery. He made many changes and introduced new ideas. Shawnee's Corn Queen and Corn King dinnerware have long been popular with collectors. Shawnee also made lobster sets under the Kenwood division.

Shawnee Corn small platter, $25.00 – 30.00; Corn cup/saucer set, $15.00 – 20.00; Corn covered casserole, $70.00 – 75.00.

Shawnee backstamp.

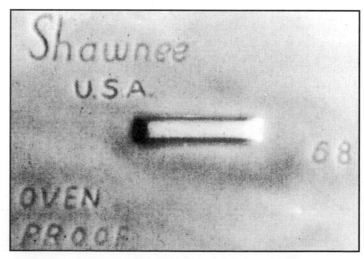

Southern Potteries

Southern Potteries was established in 1918 in the hope that the Carolina, Clinchfield, and Ohio Railroad would further encourage industries in the area. The pottery was built by Ted Owens of Minerva, Ohio. Difficulty in keeping experienced potters and the training of local people caused a couple of reorganizations of the pottery.

The hand painting on the bisque and cheap wages paid to the local help contributed to the success of the pottery. Literally thousands of pieces were sold for theater premiums in the 1940s. The ability to discard one pattern and start another, with little or no expense, was another contributing factor to Southern's success.

Southern Potteries was liquidated in the 1950s and was sold to the National Casket Company, thus ending another American pottery story. Southern Potteries began as Clinchfield Ware, became Southern Potteries, and later was better known as Blue Ridge China Company.

Many decorating companies made matching or coordinating designs to go with the hand painting done at the Southern Pottery plant.

Ted Owens of Minerva, Ohio, went to Erwin, Tennessee, about 1910 to build a Southern Potteries plant. The new plant was completed around 1918. Typical of the pottery industry, pottery workers moved to Erwin, from Ohio and West Virginia to work in the new Tennessee plant.

According to Floyd McKee in his book, "The task of keeping old potters down there and training the boys from the hills was too much for him and it had to be reorganized a couple of times."

In the beginning conventional decorated ware was produced under the Clinchfield name. Later Mr. Charles Foreman, also from Minerva, Ohio, took over the operation and it became known as Southern Potteries. The introduction of hand painting and the low wages paid to the mountain men and women made the ware affordable and popular. The ease of changing the hand-painted patterns also contributed to the success of Southern Potteries. The pottery closed in 1957. Its now famous Blue Ridge dinnerware is a wonderful example of Appalachian Mountain art.

Boxed sets today would be a real treasure to find. Blue Ridge has become extremely collectible and difficult to find. Four-place setting in original box. No price established.

Violet backstamp.

Violet platter, $25.00 – 30.00; teacup and saucer set, $14.00 – 16.00; after dinner cup/saucer, $30.00 – 35.00 set; coffee server, $50.00 – 55.00.

Palace Milady pitcher, $160.00 – 175.00.

Wild Strawberry plate, $14.00 – 16.00.

Priscilla Clinchfield plate, $16.00 – 18.00.

Sunflower teapot, $55.00 – 75.00.

Weathervane decoration, Skyline shape plate, $14.00 – 16.00.

Waltz Time small plate, $6.00 – 8.00; plate, $14.00 – 16.00; cup and saucer set, $14.00 – 16.00.

Late 1930s "Three-Toed Rabbit," Very important piece. No price established at this time.

Former decorators of the Southern Potteries identified the pieces shown. Many patterns and variations of those patterns are hand painted on a smaller variety of blanks, resulting in an almost limitless array of hand-painted patterns.

Wild Rose is the pattern shown on the Colonial blank as identified by workers.

Page 265

All 9" plates.

Row 1: Crabapple on Colonial shape, $20.00 – 25.00; Tiger Lily on Skyline shape, $20.00 – 25.00; Crabapple variant on Colonial shape, $20.00 – 25.00.

Row 2: Fruit on Colonial shape, $25.00 – 30.00; Cosmos on Skyline shape, $15.00 – 20.00; Farmhouse on Woodcrest shape, $60.00 – 65.00.

Row 3: Poppy decoration on Candlewick shape, $20.00 – 25.00; Mixed Fruit on Colonial shape, $20.00 – 25.00; Spring Garden decoration on Candlewick shape, $25.00 – 30.00.

Row 4: Plaid Fruit on Skyline shape, $20.00 – 25.00; Spring Flowers on Colonial shape, $15.00 – 20.00; Cosmos on Skyline shape, $20.00 – 25.00.

Southern Potteries Breakfast Set

Row 1: Large plate, $35.00 – 40.00; small plate, $25.00 – 30.00; teapot, $125.00 – 130.00.

Row 2: Egg cup, $30.00 – 35.00; cup/saucer set, $25.00 – 30.00; covered muffin, $125.00 – 130.00.

A variety of marks used over the years on Southern Potteries pieces.

Stangl Pottery

The Stangl Pottery had its beginning as early as 1805 as Fulper Pottery. Another larger plant was built in 1928 in Trenton, New Jersey. J. M. Stangl was president for many years and the dinnerware line is marked "Stangl."

Stangl was purchased in 1978 by the Pfaltzgraff Company. One of the Stangl dinnerware patterns, "Indian Tree," is now being made by Hartstone Potteries.

One of the most unusual patterns to come from Stangl is the hand-painted artist-signed Cactus and Cowboys. Each piece is slightly different. Three different artists sign the various Cactus and Cowboys dinnerware.

Most Stangl pieces are marked "Stangl" and many will have the pattern name included, quite a break for the collector.

Stangl Magnolia plate, $14.00 – 16.00.

Stangl backstamps.

China, Glass & Tableware, March 1963.

Orchard Song

Bittersweet

Country Garden

Fruit

Thistle

Fruit and Flowers

Sculptured Fruit, 1967.

Stetson China Company

(Also known as Stetson Pottery Company)

Louis Stetson was an immigrant from Poland who worked for his uncle in a clothing store on Chicago's Maxwell Street. Louis heard there was money to be made buying whiteware, decorating it then reselling the ware. Louis visited the Mt. Clemens Pottery with this in mind. Mt. Clemens's production was increasing at this time and they let Mr. Stetson have whiteware as a starter. The arrangement really amounted to Mt. Clemens financing Stetson's venture — a venture that proved to be a successful one for both parties. Stetson eventually took all off-selection merchandise from Mt. Clemens.

Louis Stetson brought his nephew Joe from Poland to work for him and it is said he was an even better operator than Louis. Louis passed away and Joe eventually became the owner of the Stetson operation. Stetson had been decorating the whiteware he purchased from Mt. Clemens in Chicago and the Illinois China Company in Lincoln, Illinois. In 1946 he bought the Illinois China Company. Stetson bought odd lots of decals, making his operation an even more profitable one.

Soon after buying the Illinois China Company, Stetson discontinued the use of decals and used hand painting. We know Stetson brought in decorators from both Red Wing and Southern Potteries. Some sources say the hand painting only lasted 2 – 3 years and Stetson went back to decals.

Nearly all of Stetson's later ware was sold to a Chicago brokerage firm who in turn sold the ware to grocery and furniture stores to be used as premiums. Golden Empress was one of these lines and has a wide 22-karat gold border with various decaled centers.

At one time, Stetson was the second largest employer in Lincoln. Stetson also had a plastics plant and it was at some time sold to Allied Chemical.

The Stetson China Company went out of business in 1965. The Stetson family ran a Stetson-Fostoria outlet in Lincoln, Illinois, on North Kickapoo Street. The outlet store opened in 1959 and was the brain child of Joe Stetson and his son-in-law, Burt Chudacoff. The *Lincoln Courier*, July 18, 1979, reported the final closing sale of the Stetson-Fostoria outlet store.

A November 1965 article in *China, Glass & Tableware* announced that Lincoln China Company would be closed down within a year. The plant had formerly been the Stetson operation and Stetson had sold its equipment to Allied Chemical. Allied then operated the business as Stetson Products, Plastic Division. Several top Stetson executives went with Allied and the name change to Lincoln China Company was part of the sales package deal. The Stetson name could no longer be used.

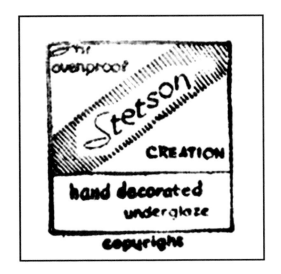

Stetson backstamps.

Stetson backstamps.

Page 273

This is a mixture of Stetson, Mt. Clemens, and Illinois China Company. Please read the company history on page 269. Stetson was a major decorator who bought from Homer Laughin, Mt. Clemens, and others.

Row 1: All 6" plates. Steps decoration on Mt. Clemens Alara shape; Suzanne decoration on Alara shape; Illinois China Company, Gold Border; Floral Border. $4.00 – 6.00 each.

Row 2: Mt. Clemens Alara shape platter, marked Stetson Mexicalis, $35.00 – 40.00; sugar (lid missing), $20.00 – 25.00; if complete, $22.00 – 28.00; 9" Alara shape 9" plate, $20.00 – 25.00. The sugar and platter are from Mt. Clemens's Old Mexico line.

Row 3: Ionic shape, Stetson's hand-decorated Cynthia line, in Sears 1949 spring and summer catalog. Cynthia decoration has a ruffled edge. 6" plate, $8.00 – 10.00; fruit/sauce bowl, $6.00 – 8.00; small mixing/utility bowl, $35.00 – 40.00.

Row 4: All Cynthia decoration. 7" square luncheon plate, $15.00 – 20.00; flat soup, $12.00 – 15.00; 6" plate, $10.00 – 12.00.

Steubenville Pottery

The Steubenville Pottery was organized in 1879 in Steubenville, Ohio. By 1881, the business had grown and the pottery was incorporated. Progress continued under the direction of W. B. Donaldson.

By 1910, The Steubenville Pottery had continued to grow and H. D. Wintringer became president of the board of directors. The Wintringer name continued to be an important name at the Steubenville operation.

The pottery closed its doors in 1959. The buildings were sold to a chemical company and the Canonsburg Pottery in Canonsburg, Pennsylvania, purchased the Steubenville molds. Some Rose Point and Adam Antique was made after 1959 and stock-on-hand was sold under the Steubenville label at Canonsburg, Pennsylvania. A line called Partio was also sold in 1965 under the Steubenville name. Woodfield and Russel Wright's American Modern line are Steubenville's most readily recognized patterns. American Modern molds were not included in the sale to Canonsburg.

In 1948, Steubenville had three lines advertised: Monticello, Steubenville, and American Modern. Steubenville's Monticello Dinnerware was an important new collection that included Pate sur Pate, available in solid colors with contrasting colors. Other Monticello lines were decorated with decals.

Woodfield

Gay and unusual is this smart leaf pattern by Steubenville. The distinctive shape of *Woodfield* will add an exciting new beauty to your tables . . . the unique pieces will add a new joy to dining. Mix them or match them in five wonderful, wonderful colors: Golden Fawn, Salmon Pink, Tropic, Rust and Dove Gray.

A DINNERWARE MASTERPIECE BY THE STEUBENVILLE POTTERY CO., STEUBENVILLE, OHIO

Woodfield as shown in advertising brochure.

Steubenville backstamp.

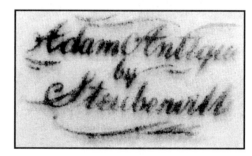

Page 275
Row 1: American Modern Seafoam green creamer, $18.00 – 20.00; Rust Woodfield bowl, $8.00 – 10.00; Woodfield Rust and Tropic green shakers, $6.00 – 8.00 each.

Row 2: Tropic Green covered sugar, $25.00 – 30.00; Rust teapot, $45.00 – 50.00; Golden Fawn creamer, $18.00 – 20.00.

Row 3: American Modern after-dinner cups and saucers, each set, $12.00 – 15.00; Dove Gray cup, $6.00 – 8.00; Tropic green snack plate, $8.00 – 10.00.

Row 4: Snack plates: Salmon pink, Rust, and Golden Fawn, $8.00 – 10.00 each.

Steubenville backstamps.

Trade publication reprint.

Taylor, Smith and Taylor Pottery

The Taylor, Smith and Taylor Pottery was founded in 1899 by C. A. Smith and Colonel John N. Taylor, using the facilities of the Taylor, Smith & Lee Pottery which had ceased operations three years earlier.

In 1903 the company was reorganized and the Taylor interests were purchased by W. L. Smith and his son, W. L. Smith, Jr. The firm remained under the ownership and management of the Smith Family until early 1973 when the plant was purchased by Anchor Hocking Corporation and became the foundation of its Pottery Division.

Taylor, Smith and Taylor began operations as a nine-kiln pottery employing approximately 50 people. In those early days, only local clays were used. Later, the company bought clays from Kentucky, Georgia, Tennessee, North Carolina, and Florida. For many years both earthen and fine china bodies were used. The china body was discontinued in the early 1970s.

The Anchor Hocking Company closed in 1981. A small crew was kept until all inventory was sold. All inventory was gone by 1982.

Dogwood

A famous Taylor, Smith and Taylor underglaze pattern that has been a firm favorite in the past decade, Dogwood is made in plain colors of red, blue, green, or brown, or is hand painted with many colors.

Underglaze prints such as Dogwood, Castle, and Spring Bouquet are printed direct from original copper engravings made exclusively for the pottery by the distinguished ceramic artist, J. Palin Thorley. Protected under the glaze of every piece of ware is an etching so fine one can see each thread-like pen strokes.

Taylor, Smith, and Taylor backstamp.

Reprinted from a 1942 Taylor, Smith and Taylor pricing book.

Lu-Ray Pastels

Lu-Ray pastels was one of Taylor, Smith and Taylor's most popular lines. Lu-Ray enjoyed a long run from the late 1930s until the early fifties. Five pastel colors make for an interesting mix or match set. Of these five colors, Windsor Blue, Persian Cream, Sharon Pink, Surf Green, and Chatham Gray, Chatham Gray is the most difficult color to find.

A 1940s Ward's catalog shows a Lu-Ray Sharon Pink pitcher and Lu-Ray Empire shape salt & pepper shakers with a pastel set called "Rainbow." Taylor, Smith and Taylor officials tell us "mixing with another shape has always been a common practice and the Rainbow name was used with several shapes over the years." Catalogs and advanced collectors have been most helpful with Lu-Ray pastels information.

All Lu-Ray pastels shown are from the collection of John Moses.

Taylor, Smith and Taylor backstamps.

Page 279
Row 1: Old style Windsor Blue footed pitcher, $75.00 – 90.00; Windsor Blue water tumbler, $20.00 – 25.00; Sharon Pink juice jug, $80.00 – 100.00; Persian Cream juice tumbler, $35.00 – 45.00; Sharon Pink cake plate (also sold with wicker handle and metal handle), $45.00 – 50.00.

Row 2: Chatham Gray 7" plate, $20.00 – 25.00; Sharon Pink gravy/sauce boat, $25.00 – 30.00; Surf Green muffin cover and 8" underplate, $70.00 – 80.00; Sharon Pink ¼-pound butter, $50.00 – 75.00; Sharon Pink egg cup, $15.00 – 20.00.

Row 3: Windsor Blue teapot and cover, $45.00 – 55.00; Persian Cream after-dinner cup and saucer set, $25.00 – 30.00; Windsor Blue covered after-dinner coffeepot, $75.00 – 80.00; Sharon Pink after-dinner creamer, $25.00 – 35.00; Windsor Blue after-dinner covered sugar, $30.00 – 40.00.

Row 1: All pieces marked "Lu-Ray": Surf Green tab-handled soup, $20.00 – 30.00; Sharon Pink after-dinner covered sugar, $80.00 – 90.00; Surf Green after-dinner coffee server, $250.00 – 300.00; Windsor Blue after-dinner creamer, $70.00 – 80.00; Sharon Pink 9" plate, Leaf decoration, $15.00 – 20.00; cream soup, Leaf decoration, $40.00 – 45.00.

Row 2: Sharon Pink 10" plate, $25.00 – 30.00; Persian Cream 8" plate, $15.00 – 20.00; 9" 1959 calendar plate, $15.00 – 20.00; tab-handled serving/utility tray, $45.00 – 50.00.

Page 281

Row 1: Leaf marked, Coral Craft decoration Sharon Pink creamer, $12.00 – 15.00; Sharon Pink Leaf decoration cup, $8.00 – 10.00; shaker with small pink flower, $6.00 – 8.00; 4" fruit bowl/saucer, $3.00 – 4.00.

Row 2: Pink Sharon Leaf decoration 9" plate, $8.00 – 10.00; Leaf cream soup, $12.00 – 15.00; Leaf gravy/sauce boat, $18.00 – 22.00.

Row 3: Chateau Buffet handled ramequin, $8.00 – 10.00; small plate standing, $6.00 – 8.00; Center cup and standing pieces from the company's Design 69 line. Cup, $6.00 – 8.00; 6" plate, $4.00 – 6.00; cereal bowl, $6.00 – 8.00.

Row 4: Green Dots 9" plate, $8.00 – 12.00; Floral Bouquet 6" plate, $3.00 – 4.00; Morningside 9" plate, $8.00 – 10.00.

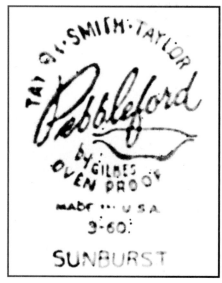

Taylor, Smith and Taylor backstamps.

Page 283

Row 1: Silhouette Laurel shape sugar, lid missing, as is, $18.00 – 20.00; complete with lid, $25.00 – 30.00; Silhouette decorated creamer, $18.00 – 20.00; Autumn Harvest Versatile line ¼-lb. covered butter, $15.00 – 18.00; unhandled Daisy sugar with lid, $12.00 – 15.00.

Row 2: Roses 2" plate, $4.00 – 6.00; Bokay after-dinner cup, $10.00 – 15.00; after-dinner coffee server, lid missing, as-is, $15.00 – 20.00; if complete, $35.00 – 45.00; Daisy 9" plate, $8.00 – 10.00.

Row 3: All 6" plates. Touch of Brown, Tulips, Bridal Flowers, and Bokay, $4.00 – 6.00 each.

Row 4: 1960 calendar plate, Laurel shape, sold to theaters and retail stores, used as gifts, $8.00 – 10.00; Silhouette decoration 9" plate, Laurel shape, $10.00 – 15.00; Autumn Harvest plate, Versatile shape, Ever-Yours collection, late 1950s – 1960s, large-volume supermarket promotional pattern, $8.00 – 10.00.

Taylor, Smith and Taylor backstamps.

Vistosa (1938 – Early 1940s)

Taylor, Smith and Taylor's response to Homer Laughlin China's Fiesta is thought to be Vistosa. Pie crust edges are in nearly the same colors as Homer Laughlin's Fiesta. Vistosa came in Mango Red, cobalt blue, light green, and deep yellow. Important Vistosa pieces known to exist, but not pictured, are a 12" footed salad bowl and sauceboat.

Row 1: Cobalt blue Vistosa 9" plate, $18.00 – 20.00; yellow 11" chop plate, $35.00 – 40.00; yellow cup/saucer set, $16.00 – 20.00.

Row 2: Vistosa Mango Red creamer, $25.00 – 30.00; yellow sugar and cover, $40.00 – 45.00; cobalt blue after-dinner cup/saucer set, $40.00 – 50.00; green egg cup, $40.00 – 50.00.

Row 3: Yellow ball jug, $75.00 – 100.00; cobalt blue shaker, $8.00 – 10.00; six-cup Mango Red teapot, $100.00 – 120.00; Mango Red shaker, $10.00 – 12.00.

Vistosa from the colllection of John Moses.

Universal Potteries, Inc.

The first known pottery in Niles, Ohio, was the Bradshaw Pottery, in business from 1902 – 1910. Frank Sebring purchased the Bradshaw plant and incorporated it under the name of Tritt in 1912. Tritt was a brother-in-law and the business never quite came up to Mr. Sebring's expectations. He sold the Tritt operation about 1921 and kept the molds.

In 1921, Mr. Ahrendts, Mr. Stevens, and Mr. Gilmer purchased the property with Mr. Chester Wardeska, secretary of the newly-formed Crescent China Company. About 1923 it was necessary to change the name of the Crescent China Company to The Atlas China Company due to an infringement claim based on prior registration.

The Atlas China Company remained in business until fire destroyed it in 1925. The Atlas plant in Niles was rebuilt and modernized following the 1925 fire. It continued to operate until nearly 1928. At that time, it was decided to consolidate all operations in the Cambridge factory and that plant was enlarged.

The Oxford Pottery was formed and financed by a group of Cambridge people in 1913. It was spearheaded by several former employees of the Guernseyware Company. Their product was a line of brown kitchenware, such as teapots, beanpots, and custards, made chiefly from crude red clay mined from the land surrounding the plant and owned by the company. The venture was successful from the start, but the business never expanded and after the loss of one of the chief executives and a year not up to standard, some of the stockholders were vulnerable to an offer for their stock by Mr. Ahrendts, and he succeeded in acquiring control.

The Globe China Company was organized in 1925 with the same three men who started the Crescent China Company in 1921. The Atlas Company decided to consolidate all its operations, under the name Atlas-Globe. Atlas-Globe never filed for bankruptcy, but in the 1930s worked out a creditor's agreement for the orderly liquidation of the assets with the Oxford Company acting as agent. At the same time, Oxford amended its charter, changing the name to Universal, increasing the capital structure, and purchasing the Atlas-Globe properties.

The original Oxford plant facilities were used in the production of ovenware in the early years of Universal and it was not unusual to call its ware Oxford ware. When this plant was converted to ceramic tile in 1956, the trademark for Oxford was adopted.

Plant #2 was converted into a wall tile manufacturing company in 1956. Plant #3 ceased operations in 1957, and Plant #1 closed in 1960, ending the dinnerware industry in Cambridge, Ohio.

Universal Potteries, Incorporated, Cambridge, Ohio, was formed in 1934 through the acquisition of the old Atlas-Globe plant properties by The Oxford Pottery Company. The Oxford organization was a local organization that amended its charter to provide for the increased investment and property expansion.

The resulting company consisted of three manufacturing plants, one located at Niles, Ohio, and subsequently dismantled. The other two remaining plants were enlarged and improved and were known as Plant 1 and Plant 2 of Universal Potteries, Inc. During 1947 the plant embarked on an expansion program that included a brand new facility completed in 1948, known as Plant 3.

Universal's Ballerina and Ballerina Mist color glazes, both plain and decorated, have best distinguished the company. Universal used a detergent-resistant decal called permacel.

Universal also added distinction to its line by the versatility of its products as evidenced by the complete assortment of cooking ware and "guaranteed ovenproof" refrigerator items.

Universal Potteries, Incorporated, had 200 employees in 1934 and 650 in 1956. Without exception, managers and supervisors of Universal Potteries, Incorporated, came up through the ranks of the factory force.

Some of the backstamps used on Universal shapes over the years.

Cattail

Cattail is a very popular pattern with collectors. A Universal executive tells us that the Cattail decal was made up for an East Liverpool pottery. The name of the pottery is not known but it did not use the decal.

Universal used the Cattail design on its Camwood shape, Old Holland shape, and Laurella shape (possibly other shapes). Please keep in mind "exclusive" meant only exclusive shapes with a particular decal to be sold only to one buyer.

One of the interesting facets of Cattail is the variety of pieces to be found aside from the different shapes mentioned above. Glass, linens, tinware, and even a kitchen table make up the extensive pieces available for the Cattail collector.

The ad from the *Needlecraft* magazine shown on the opposite page is from 1934 and the maker is unknown at this time.

A Cattail jug with reamer has created quite a stir, both with dinnerware collectors and reamer collectors. Watch for it!

Universal backstamps.

Cattail Pattern 32 PIECES

WILL YOU ACCEPT THIS 32-PIECE SET AS A GIFT?

Exceptionally striking pattern.   Extraordinarily low offer.

This Set *Given* for only *Twelve* subscriptions to Needlecraft at 50 cents each

THIS set consists of:

6 *Large Plates*

6 *Small Plates*

6 *Cups*

6 *Saucers*

6 *Oatmeals*

1 *Platter*

1 *Round Vegetable Dish*

THIS delightful new pattern was perhaps designed by some city artist who experienced a longing for the open spaces of his boyhood home. At any rate he got exactly the delightful and effective charm of graceful and colorful cattails which he has effectively placed on the white background of these lovely dishes. The shape of the dishes is most charming and the design of the border embossed in the ware (not painted on) adds tremendously to the colorful decorative effect of the main motif.

The color-scheme is simple—red and black on the white background. We guarantee you will love it on sight.

BARGAIN OFFER—This offer is open to anyone who reads this advertisement but it is guaranteed for 30 days only. We cannot tell how long this bargain offer can last in the face of steadily increasing prices. So act now. Collect only 12 yearly subscriptions to Needlecraft Magazine at 50 cents each. Send us the $6 collected with the names and addresses of the subscribers.

Gift Subscriptions do not count. You must be prepared to say that none of the subscriptions except your own were paid for by you. Each subscriber will receive this magazine one year and you will receive this 32-piece set of dishes sent carried charges all prepaid and guaranteed against breakage in delivery. Order by name and by Gift No. 4444.

NEEDLECRAFT, Augusta, Maine

This Cattail is not Universal's. Reprinted from a 1930s *Needlecraft* Magazine.

Cattail juice tumbler, hard to find,
marked Universal, $35.00 – 40.00.

1940 Sears catalog reprint.

Page 291

Row 1: Cattail saucer on Old Holland shape, marked "Wheelock," $6.00 – 8.00; three styles of shakers, $12.00 – 14.00 each; fruit/sauce dish on Old Holland shape, $4.00 – 6.00.

Row 2: Individual teapot, $40.00 – 45.00; batter jug, $100.00 – 125.00; Laurella shape creamer, $16.00 – 18.00.

Row 3: Server, $20.00 – 25.00; tablecloth, $100.00 – 125.00; glass pitcher, $65.00 – 70.00; glass tumbler, $18.00 – 22.00; salad set, bowl, fork, and spoon, complete, $55.00 – 65.00.

Row 4: Laurella shape 10" plate, $8.00 – 10.00; serving plate, $20.00 – 24.00.

H 89c
J 39c
K 65c
L $1.19
M 69c
P $1.79
Matched economy Pantryware—bright cattail design
The pantryware for the thrifty buyer. Not equal to our finest Maid of Honor Pantryware above, yet it is well made of steel with a smooth white lithographed outside finish and a protective rust-resistant inside finish.
H Step-on Can. 10-quart capacity. About 13 inches high. Painted inset.
11 J 2803M—Shipping weight 4 lbs. 3 oz...89c
J Oval Wastebasket. Bright white with red inside. 12⅝ inches high. Straight sides.
11 J 2805M—Shipping weight 2 lbs. 2 oz...39c
K Cake Cover and Tray. 5¼ inches high, 10¼-inch diameter cover.
11 J 2804M—Shipping weight 2 lbs. 2 oz.........65c
L Double Compartment Bread Box. 2 doors. 11¾ inches high. Lower shelf about 12x12⅝ in.
11 J 02801M—Shipping weight 6 pounds........ $1.19
M Single Compartment Bread Box. 13⅝x9⅝x6 in.
11 J 2802M—Shipping weight 3 pounds.........69c
N 4-piece Canister Set. Sizes 4⅞ in. high by 4⅛-in. diam.; 5⅝x5 in., 6⅜x6 in., 7⅜x7⅛ in.
11 J 2800M—Shipping weight 2 lbs. 9 oz......Set 65c
Maid of Honor Kitchen Scale
P The neatest, most attractive kitchen scale we have ever seen at this low price. Very handy, too, for weighing articles up to 24 pounds. Convenient for weighing packages to be mailed. Useful on farms, in hotels and in city homes. (Not legal for use in trade.) Made of heavy gauge steel painted white, with attractive cattail design. Clear plastic dial face. Figures are stamped legibly on revolving white dial. Easy adjustment makes constant accuracy possible. Height 6¾ inches. Weighing surface 6x6 inches; base 6¼x6¼ inches. A good buy at this low price.
11 J 7851M—Shipping weight 4 pounds......

Cat-Tail Kitchenware . . . Guaranteed Oven and Craze Proof
9-Piece Refrigerator Set (A, B, and C)
A B C D E F G H J K
• Created by skilled designers for kitchen beauty and space efficiency.
• Perky red and black cat-tails and red lines decorate every piece.
• Finest quality American semi-porcelain with ivory color glaze.
• Guaranteed against crazing—every piece is ovenproof . . . acid resistant.
• Tested by Sears and independent laboratories . . . to give tops in wear.
• Priced for real savings. See Page 666 for Matching Cat-tail Dinnerware.
9-Piece Refrigerator Set
$2.79 Set
Set of: (A) 3 Covered Jars, 4, 5, 6 in. diam.; 3, 3¾, 4¾ in. high. (B) Covered Casserole, 8¼ in. diam.; 4⅜ in. high. 2 qt. cap. (C) Canteen Jug with stopper. Cap. 1 qt. 7 oz. Ht., 7½ in. to fit refrigerators. Shpg. wt., 12 lbs.
35 H 5152M—9-Pc. Set.................. $2.79
(A) 6-Pc. Ice Box Jar Set
$1.19 Set
Store food in covered jars! Set of 3 covered jars, 4, 5, 6 in. diam., 3, 3¾, 4¾ in. high. Genuine space savers. Stack conveniently for storing in refrigerator or pantry. Shpg. wt., 5 lbs. 8 oz.
35 H 5145M—Set...................... $1.19
(C) Canteen Jug
Only 85c
Keep juices and water fresh and cool! 7½ in. high to fit refrigerator. 1-qt. 7 oz. cap. Cork stopper. Shipping weight, 2 lbs. 8 oz.
35 H 5041M.............85c
(D) Handy Pitcher
55c
It'll come to the table every day with milk, water, or even waffle batter. 1 qt. 5 oz. cap. 6 in. high. Shpg. wt., 1 lb. 8 oz.
35 H 5151M............55c
(E) Ice-Lipped Pitcher
95c
Just what you want for iced drinks! Ice-lip assures drip-less pouring. 5⅝-in. high; 2-qt. 10-oz. cap. Wt., 2 lbs. 12 oz.
35 H 5149M...........95c
(F) Giant Cooky Jar
$1.35
Even the heartiest cookie-eating family finds this jar plenty big! Full one-gallon capacity. 9 in. high. Shpg. wt., 9 lbs.
35 H 5153M......... $1.35
(G) 2-Pc. Pie Set
57c
Bake and serve your pie in the same dish. Deep pie plate. 10-in. diam. with easy-out server. Shpg. wt., 2 lbs. 12 oz.
35 H 5036M...........57c
(H) 6 Custard Cups
69c Set
Bake custards, mold salad or serve pudding in them! Large 6-oz. cap. 3⅜ in. diam. Shpg. wt., 2 lbs. 12 oz.
35 H 5150M—Six for...69c
(K) Covered Casserole
$1.09
Serve food piping hot! Snug cover with knob. 8¼-in. diam.; 4½ in. high. 1¾-qt. cap. Shipping weight, 4 lbs. 8 oz.
35 H 5148M......... $1.09
(J) 4-Pc. Range Set
85c
Keep your pepper and salt on the stove! Large salt and pepper shakers, 4 in. high. Covered lard jar, 3 in. high.
35H5143M—Shpg.wt., 3 lbs..85c

46-piece matching Breakfast Set
• 46 pieces with matched black and vermilion cat-tail decorations
• 5-Pc. solid oak Breakfast Set
• 32-Pc. set of semi-porcelain dishes
• Gay 9-pc. cotton luncheon set
$23.89 Cash 46-Pc. Set $3 Down
Extension Table top, 42x30 inches; opens to 52x30 inches. Legs bolt on. Chair seats, 15x14 inches. Height of back from seat, 17½ inches. Pearl white or fawn tan. State finish. Shipped from near Louisville, Ky.
1 LM 8637F—Complete 46-piece Breakfast Outfit. Shipping weight, 120 pounds.................... $23.89
1 LM 2527F—5 Pcs. Table, 4 chairs. Shpg.wt., 100 lbs. 18.98
Chair only. Shipping weight, 13 pounds. Each.. 2.85

Inexpensive pantryware pieces advertised in a 1940s Sears catalog include 10 qt., 3" high Cattail step-on garbage can, 12" high oval wastebasket, cake cover, double breadbox, single breadbox, four-piece round canister set, and kitchen scales. In the 1941 Sears catalog there is a breakfast set, with choice of enameled white hardwood or solid oak Fawn Tan finish. The table and seats of the chairs are decorated with black and Vermillion Cattail. Included in the breakfast outfit were a 32-piece set of Cattail dinnerware and a nine-piece cotton luncheon set, all 46 pieces for $19.98. In 1942 the nine-piece cotton luncheon set did not have the cattails; it appears to have a stripe around the edge.

Accessory pieces shown are from a 1940s Sears catalog.

Row 1: Glass spice set with red metal lids, complete with metal holder, $55.00 – 60.00 set; sugar, lid missing, as is, $8.00 – 10.00; if complete, $18.00 – 24.00; glass spice set, metal frame missing, spice jars, $8.00 – 10.00 each.

Row 2: Ice-lipped pitcher, 2 quart, $35.00 – 40.00; jug with cork stopper, $35.00 – 40.00; utility pitcher, $18.00 – 20.00.

Row 3: Canteen pitcher, $25.00 – 30.00; another style shaker, $10.00 – 12.00; part of three-piece utility bowl set, larger bowl, $18.00 – 22.00; small bowl, $15.00 – 18.00; large cookie jar (may not be correct lid or lid may have been redesigned), $55.00 – 60.00.

Row 4: Platter, $18.00 – 22.00; 7" plate, $2.00 – 4.00; covered 1-lb. butter dish, $70.00 – 75.00; metal kitchen scales, as is, $50.00 – 60.00; if mint condition, $95.00 – 100.00.

Row 1: Hollyhocks salad bowl, $25.00 – 30.00; Rose bowl, made for Sears, $20.00 – 25.00; blue Criss-Cross decoration bowl, marked "Made especially for Blair," $25.00 – 30.00.

Row 2: Holland Rose decoration on Old Holland shape 6" plate, $8.00 – 10.00; Holland Rose decoration on Old Holland shape 4" sauce/fruit bowl, $4.00 – 6.00; Holland Rose decoration on Laurella shape 9" plate, $10.00 – 12.00.

Rambler Rose or Iris

Page 295

Row 1: Rambler Rose decoration 6" plate, $4.00 – 5.00; shaker, $10.00 – 15.00; gravy/sauce boat, $20.00 – 25.00.

Row 2: Rambler Rose utility jug, $25.00 – 28.00; flat soup, $12.00 – 15.00; 9" plate, $8.00 – 10.00.

Row 3: Iris decoration jug, $40.00 – 45.00; stack set and covers, $70.00 – 75.00 set; covered casserole, $45.00 – 50.00.

Row 4: Iris decoration pie baker, $25.00 – 30.00; canteen refrigerator jug, $30.00 – 35.00; 9" plate, $10.00 – 12.00.

Page 297

Row 1: Largo decoration sugar, as is (lid missing), $12.00 – 15.00; salt and pepper, $8.00 – 10.00 each; small utility bowls, $10.00 – 12.00 and $8.00 – 10.00.

Row 2: Largo decoration 7" luncheon plate, $6.00 – 8.00; 6" dessert plate, $4.00 – 6.00; 10" pie baker, $15.00 – 20.00.

Row 3: Red Poppy decoration 11½" utility plate, $12.00 – 15.00; 6" plates, $4.00 – 6.00 each.

Row 4: Windmill decoration utility bowl and cover, $30.00 – 35.00; shaker, $12.00 – 15.00; Fruit and Flowers utility tray, $12.00 – 15.00.

The Largo pattern was made for the S.B. Davis Company and came in a wide variety of pieces. Red Poppy was sold to department stores and catalog stores. Both patterns are from the 1940s.

Universal Potteries backstamps.

Woodvine, Universal Potteries' most popular "booster" line, was used as a premium line for grocery stores on a coupon basis to stimulate business. Many of Universal's patterns were boosters in the 1930s and 1940s.

Page 299
All Woodvine decoration.
Row 1: Gravy/sauce boat, $18.00 – 20.00; salt and pepper shakers, $12.00 – 15.00 each; sugar and cover, $20.00 – 25.00; creamer, $15.00 – 20.00.

Row 2: Utility jar and cover, $35.00 – 40.00; gravy boat liner or pickle/relish dish, $10.00 – 12.00; small fruit/sauce bowl, $4.00 – 6.00.

Row 3: 9" plate, $10.00 – 12.00; oval vegetable bowl, $12.00 – 15.00; square luncheon plate, $10.00 – 12.00.

Row 4: Cup/saucer set, $12.00 – 15.00 set; flat soup bowl, $8.00 – 10.00; utility tray, $15.00 – 18.00.

Universal backstamp.

Page 301

Row 1: Blue and white "God Bless America" syrup pitcher, $55.00 – 60.00; blue and white refrigerator ware made for Montgomery Ward in the 1940s: covered jar, $10.00 – 15.00; covered jar, $15.00 – 20.00; covered jar, $25.00 – 30.00.

Row 2: Blue and white canteen jug, $35.00 – 40.00; cookie jar, Mod Flower decoration, lid missing, $35.00 – 40.00; if complete, $55.00 – 60.00; Stylized Rose coffee server, $35.00 – 40.00.

Row 3: Cattail coffee base, $45.00 – 50.00; Woodvine utility jug, $30.00 – 35.00; Cattail coffee base, $45.00 – 50.00.

Row 4: Canteen refrigerator jugs, various decorations, $40.00 – 45.00 each.

Several American potteries made plates and bowls to fit chrome and aluminum frames. This Grecian Urn decal is on Universal's Laurella shape and in a Farberware frame. A *House Beautiful* ad from summer of 1940 shows the same plate in a different style frame. $35.00 – 40.00.

Calico Fruit

Calico Fruit is a popular pattern with collectors and was sold in the forties in department and catalog stores. It is difficult to find table pieces such as saucers and plates with good bright decals. Calico Fruit had matching tinware and glass condiment sets as shown in the 1946 – 1947 Ward's catalog below.

Semi-porcelain Dinnerware

(A) TO (L) CALICO FRUIT OVENWARE. Semi-Porcelain guaranteed absolutely heatproof, cold-proof and acid-resisting. Matches Calico Fruit Dinnerware described below.

(A) 86 C 7720L—RANGE SET. 4-in. Jar, 4-in. Salt and Pepper. Ship. wt. 4 lbs........... 98c
(B) 86 C 7728L—COVERED REFRIGERATOR JUG. 3-pt. capacity. Ship. wt. 3 lbs........... $1.15
(C) 86 C 7729L—3-COMPARTMENT PLATE. 10-in. diameter. Ship. wt. 2 lbs................. 59c
(D) 86 C 7718L—3-JAR REFRIGERATOR SET. 4-in., 5-in., 6-in. diameters. Ship. wt. 6 lbs.... $1.39
(E) 86 C 7717L—3-Pc. MIXING BOWL SET. 6¼-in., 7½-in., 9-in. diameters. Ship. wt. 9 lbs. 1.39

Page 303

All Calico Fruit decoration.

Row 1: 6" plate, $12.00 – 15.00; salt and pepper shakers, $15.00 – 18.00 each; saucer (decal faded), $2.00 – 3.00; if bright decal, $4.00 – 6.00.

Row 2: Utility tray 11½", $25.00 – 30.00; 7" plate, $10.00 – 12.00; 9" plate, as is, $8.00 – 10.00; if not faded, $12.00 – 15.00.

Row 3: Custard cup, 5 oz. capacity, $6.00 – 8.00; refrigerator set, three jars and covers, 4", $15.00 – 18.00; 5", $18.00 – 24.00; 6", $25.00 – 30.00.

Row 4: Covered jug, 3 quart capacity, $45.00 – 50.00; small fruit/sauce bowl, $12.00 – 18.00; vegetable bowl, $18.00 – 28.00; utility jug, $45.00 – 50.00.

From Universal — these new, fast - selling *Ballerina* Specialty Sets!

16-Pc. Barbecue Set. 8 French Casseroles. 8 Coffee Mugs. Forest Green, Chartreuse, Dove Grey, Burgundy Colored Glazes; also in decorated patterns. Retail $14.39

17-Pc. Beverage Set. 1 Ice Lip Jug. 8 Tumblers, 8 Coasters. Forest Green, Chartreuse, Dove Grey, Burgundy Colored Glazes; also in decorated patterns. Retail $9.95

18-Pc. After Dinner Coffee Service. 1 A.D. Coffee Server, 8 A.D. Cups, 8 A.D. Saucers. Forest Green, Chartreuse, Dove Grey, Burgundy Colored Glazes; also in decorated patterns. Retail $8.49

18-Pc. Tea Set. 1 Teapot, 8 Tea Cups, 8 Tea Saucers. Forest Green, Chartreuse, Dove Grey, Burgundy Colored Glazes; also in decorated patterns. Retail $8.95

Smart, practical — moderately priced! These are the come-ons that make Ballerina colored glaze specialty sets hot sellers from the moment you put them on display. And they're *packaged for resale*, solid-color or assorted — ideal gifts for brides, Mother's Day and other gift occasions. See them at the Pittsburgh show . . . you'll want *all four for your store!*

Universal Potteries, Inc.
Three Modern Plants • Cambridge, Ohio

Representatives
Paul Goldwyn, Room 308-310
225 Fifth Ave., New York City
C. B. Jacoby, P. O. Box 14022, Houston 21, Texas
A. E. Miller, 1581-B Merchandise Mart, Chicago, Illinois
L. E. Heiser, Box 236, Tiffin, Ohio
Robert Snyder, RD 4, Salem, Ohio
F. W. Kasper, Gate 14, Lakewood, Crystal Lake, Ill.
Mrs. H. W. Becker, 515 Kinloch Building
St. Louis, Missouri
J. A. Wentz, Space 284 Western Merchandise Mart
1355 Market St., San Francisco, California
Russell M. Stoakes, 94 So. Greer
Memphis 11, Tennessee
Perry Karasek, 1528 42nd St.
Belview Heights, Birmingham, Ala.

Canadian Representative
Sidney Druckman, 79 Wellington St., Toronto, Ontario

Advertisement from trade publication for Universal Potteries.

Ballerina Shape — Colored Glazes

Ballerina was one of Universal's most popular shapes. It was made in solid color glazes and a variety of decals on an ivory glaze.

The four original colors were Periwinkle Blue, Jade Green, Jonquil Yellow, and Dove Grey. Chartreuse and Forest Green were added in 1949. In 1950, designer Charles Cobelle created five exclusive new patterns for Universal's Ballerina shape. Advertised as "Modern designs with a touch of the abstract," the five new patterns were Painted Desert, Mermaid, Passy, Gloucester Fisherman, and The Fountain.

A 1951 ad lists four colored glazes on Ballerina: Forest Green, Jonquil Yellow, Chartreuse, and Dove Grey. In 1955, Pink and Charcoal were added to the Ballerina line. Pink and Charcoal were "high-fashion" colors for 1955. Also in 1955 a big promotion was announced for Moss Rose on Ballerina, but the ad does not state that Moss Rose is a new item. Another 1955 Ballerina ad lists Forest Green, Chartreuse, Burgundy, Dove Grey, Pink, and Charcoal as basic colored glazes. Ballerina was also available in other "decorated motifs" including the ever-popular Moss Rose pattern.

Ballerina Mist was another popular line for Universal. The body of the ware is a "wispy blue-green" with decals.

Row 1: Chartreuse 10" plate, $10.00 – 15.00; Burgundy salad bowl, $15.00 – 20.00; Forest Green egg cup, $15.00 – 20.00; light green 9" plate, $6.00 – 8.00.

Row 2: Forest green sugar and cover, $15.00 – 20.00; turquoise creamer, $10.00 – 15.00; Dove Grey gravy/sauce boat, $10.00 – 15.00; pink cup, $8.00 – 10.00; green shaker, $6.00 – 8.00.

Row 1: Red and White kitchenware from the collection of Greg Ciccolo. Bean Pot with cover, $35.00 – 40.00; syrup pitcher, $35.00 – 40.00; six-cup teapot, $40.00 – 45.00; shaker, $10.00 – 12.00; ball jug, $60.00 – 75.00.

Row 2: Circus decoration spoon, $30.00 – 35.00; shaker, $6.00 – 8.00; six-cup teapot, $55.00 – 60.00; two-cup utility jug, $25.00 – 30.00.

Row 3: Broadway Rose plate, Atlas Globe mark, $8.00 – 10.00; Blue Oxford ware 8 oz. mug, $20.00 – 25.00; green water jug, $40.00 – 50.00; utility bowl, $10.00 – 15.00; green individual bean pot, $8.00 – 12.00.

Warwick China Company

The Warwick China Company was founded in 1887 in Wheeling, West Virginia, to make semi-porcelain table and toilet wares. The first backstamp was a helmet and crossed swords adopted about 1892 for making novelty items. The Warwick China Company is best known for its specialty items which are widely sought after by collectors. The child's set pictured below is dated 1944.

Row 1: Plate, $12.00 – 15.00; individual size teapot, $40.00 – 45.00

Row 2: Sugar and cover, $20.00 – 25.00; creamer, $18.00 – 20.00; cup/saucer set, $12.00 – 15.00.

Warwick China backstamp.

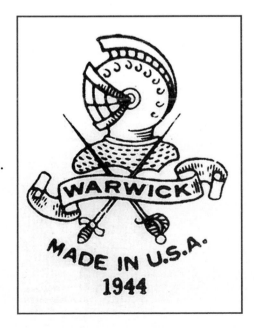

Western Stoneware

The Western Stoneware was formed in April 1906, expressly for the manufacture of stoneware items. Stoneware is made from a natural clay that requires no other minerals. Real stoneware factories are by necessity located near natural clay deposits. A high temperature is used in the firing (2290° F). Real stoneware is an excellent ware for baking and large pieces are excellent insulators, keeping food hot or cold for an indefinite period.

In 1954, Eva Zeisel developed for Monmouth Pottery a line of "nearly 50 new shapes" and 15 new patterns of highly vitrified stoneware. Three solid glaze colors, in both matte and glossy finish, also came in hand-decorated pieces. They were described by Walter Browder in an article in *Crockery and Glass Journal* as "a basic dinnerware line with basic serving pieces in classically quiet and simple shapes ... but there is a surprise in a second serving line of humorous bird shapes."

Western Stoneware was also the maker of the now famous Marcrest line of stoneware made for the Marcrest Company. Marcrest was a premium or booster item for service stations, grocery stores, and other businesses in the 1950s.

Advertisement form trade paper, date unknown.

Marcrest cookie jar, $45.00 – 50.00; snack plate, cup missing, $8.00 – 10.00.

Eva Zeisel pieces are very desirable to collectors and command high prices. No prices have been established for these unusual Monmouth pieces.

Glossary

Acid gold - a type of dinnerware decoration in which the design is acid-etched into the body, then painted with liquid gold, which is fired on and burnished.

Baker - a vegetable or serving dish, open and often oval in shape.

Basaltware - unglazed stoneware, usually black, with a dull gloss.

Batch - the precise mixture of clay and other ingredients which, by heat processing, is transformed into hard clay ware.

Bisque (or biscuit) - the porous clay after the first firing.

Bisque fire - the first firing or baking, which hardens a dinnerware piece into its final shape.

Blank - an undecorated piece, usually one to be subjected to further processing.

Body - composite materials that make up clay.

Body and paste - the composite materials from which potter's clay is made.

Bone china - a specific type of fine china manufactured primarily in England. The body contains a high proportion of bone ash to develop greater translucency, whiteness, and strength. Like fine china, it is made primarily for the retail trade.

Bright gold - A liquid gold paint decoration which, when fired, comes out bright and therefore requires no burnishing (polishing).

Burnished gold - a more expensive gold dinnerware or glassware decoration that comes out of the kiln dull and must be rubbed up to a shine.

Casting - process where liquid clay is poured into a mold and allowed to set, forming a hollow piece.

Ceramics - all products made from clay.

China - a thin, translucent, vitrified body, which is generally developed in two firings: first, at a relatively high temperature to mature the purest of raw materials; and second, to develop the high gloss of the covering glaze. This term is generally used interchangeably with the word porcelain.

Compote (or comport) - a footed or stemmed dish varying in height, size, and bowl shape, sometimes covered, used for serving candy, jelly, nuts, bon bons, etc.

Cooking ware - a broad term applied to earthenware, porcelain, and china where the shapes are designed for cooking or baking as well as serving. It has a smooth, glazed surface, is strong, and is resistant to thermal shock.

Coupe shaped - a plate curved upward at the edge, lacking a shoulder.

Crackled ware - clay ware or glassware on which the surface is marked by a network of tiny cracks deliberately induced for decorative effect by sudden cooling.

Craze - tiny cracks caused by the difference in contracting of the body and glaze.

Crockery - a term, often synonymous with earthenware, used to describe a porous opaque body for domestic use. Because of its permeability, it is normally glazed.

Cruet - any stoppered bottle that can be used for oil, vinegar, or other liquid dressing.

Decalcomania (or decal) - a special design-bearing sheet used in dinnerware decoration. The sheet is first applied to a piece of ware. The paper is then removed, resulting in the transfer of the decoration to the ware. Subsequent firing makes it permanent.

Dipping - process where china is dipped in liquid glaze, prior to second firing.

Dresden - a white china generally very heavily decorated, originally developed in Dresden, Germany.

Earthenware - a type of clay ware fired at comparatively low temperatures, producing a heavy, porous body that is opaque, not as strong as china, and lacking resonance. Because earthenware is generally in the low and medium price brackets and lends itself to a variety of decorative styles and methods, it is well suited for everyday use.

Embossing - a raised or molded decoration produced either in the mold or formed separately and applied before firing.

Engobe - a type of decoration in which white or colored slip, or liquid clay, is applied over the body of the ware.

Epergne - an ornamental table piece having two or more arms and designed to hold flowers, candles, and, recently, candies, nuts, and other tidbits.

Etching - a decoration on glassware or clay ware eaten into the ware by acid. Either of two methods, needle etching or plate etching, may be used to apply the decoration.

Faience - originally a type of French-made pottery, the term is used today to refer to a fine glazed earthenware usually bearing colorful decoration.

Firing - a baking process under carefully controlled temperatures to which all ceramic ware is subjected for hardening, strengthening, and fusing together its various ingredients.

Flatware - plates or platters of any size.

Flux - a material that aids the melting and fusion of ceramic ingredients under heat. The most commonly used fluxes in dinnerware manufacture are feldspar and bone ash.

Gadroon edge - a molded dinnerware border design which resembles braided rope.

Glaze - a glass layer covering a ceramic product before the article is baked until the coating becomes hard and permanent.

Glost firing - dinnerware's second firing, the purpose of which is to harden and set the glaze. Temperatures are generally lower than those of the first, or bisque, firing.

Glost kiln - oven for baking glazed pieces to harden the glaze.

Graffito or Sgraffito - a design scratched in the glaze to show background color, which is later reglazed and retired.

Green ware - unfinished clay ware which has not been fired.

Ground-lay - an underglaze dinnerware decoration generally taking the form of wide borders of dark colors such as maroon, deep blue, etc. The decorating process consists of dusting the powdered color onto an oil coating.

Hollowware (or hollow ware) - cups, bowls, pitchers, etc.

Hotel ware - a heavy china dinnerware made specifically for use in hotels, institutions, and restaurants. Hotel ware is stronger than china for home use, but lacks the translucency and delicacy of china.

Intaglio - decoration in which the design is sunk beneath the surface of the piece. It is the opposite of embossing.

Ironstone - a historic term for durable English stoneware. The composition and properties are similar to porcelain, except that the body is not translucent and is off-white. In more recent times, this term has been used to describe a number of other products.

Jasper - a stoneware body, either white or colored, noteworthy for its fine, soft finish. This type of ware was first developed by Josiah Wedgwood and its best known form today is the popular blue and white ware by Wedgwood.

Jigger - machine on which plates are made.

Jolley - cup-making machine.

Kaolin - a pure, white, top-grade clay used in making fine china.

Kiln - the oven in which dinnerware is fired or baked. Pottery workers pronounce the word as if it were spelled without the "n."

Limoges - French porcelain produced in the vicinity of Limoges, France.

Lining - a dinnerware decoration, either machine- or hand-applied, consisting of one or several parallel lines running around the outer edge of a plate.

Lug soup - a soup plate with two projecting pieces on opposite sides of the rim by which the plate is carried.

Luster - a ceramic glaze coating, metallic in nature, which gives the finished piece an iridescent effect.

Majolica - a type of Italian pottery glazed with tin enamel and generally decorated in rich colors.

Mat finish - a flat glaze finish without gloss. The first word is usually misspelled "matte."

Mold - form used for shaping hollow ware pieces.

Mold marks - ridges on clayware or glassware indicating the points at which the mold that formed a piece was separated for removal of the ware.

Nappy - in dinnerware, a round vegetable dish. A glassware nappy, however, is any round or square dish from fruit size up, used for various serving purposes.

Open stock - an approach to dinnerware retailing in which the ware is sold in individual pieces or small groups rather than in complete, predetermined composition or sets. Implied, also, is the fact that patterns offered in open stock will be available for an indefinite period following their introduction.

Ovenware - clay ware that is able to withstand the heat of a kitchen oven without damage, thus permitting a homemaker to prepare oven-cooked food in it and then use it for table service. Such ware is usually of casual design and features bright colors.

Overglaze decoration - design applied to clay ware after it has been fired and glazed. Because they are not subjected to high temperatures, the colors in overglaze decoration tend to be more vivid than those in underglaze designs.

Parian - a fine, unglazed porcelain developed in England, so named because it is said to resemble marble from the Greek island of Paros.

Paste - the mixture from which dinnerware is made. The two basic types are soft paste, which includes a high percentage of powdered glass, and hard paste, which is a mixture of kaolin, flint, and feldspar.

Pate Sur Pate - ornamentation made by painting paste upon paste until the desired thickness is obtained.

Pin marks - small depressions on the underside of a glazed piece left by the pins which support it in the kiln as it is fired. Although they are usually polished off, the marks cannot be completely eradicated.

Place setting - usually five (although sometimes four or six) matched pieces of dinnerware for setting a single place at a table. Higher priced ware is generally offered in such a group to keep the cost at a comparatively popular level.

Porcelain - a hard, translucent clay ware body that differs from china only in the manufacturing process. In all other respects the two are so much alike that the terms are generally used interchangeably.

Potter's wheel - a round platform, rotated either mechanically or manually, upon which the potter throws, or forms, a circular shape. The device originated in ancient times.

Pottery - as a generic name, pottery includes all fired clay ware. As a specific name, pottery describes the low porous body ware which is generally colored. The term is properly applied to the clay products of primitive peoples, or to decorated art products made of unrefined clays and by unsophisticated methods.

Ceramic products acquire strength through the application of heat. The chemical composition of the materials used determines, with the heat applied, the strength, porosity, and vitrification of the fired product. Primitive pottery, often baked in the sun and composed of one or more unrefined clays, had little strength and was quite porous.

Quimper ware - colorful French-made pottery of a peasant character which takes its name from the town of Quimper.

Reject - a piece of ware withheld from shipment because of an imperfection that prevents it from meeting first-quality standards.

Restaurant china - a unique American blending of fine china and porcelain designed and engineered specifically for use in commercial operations. The body was developed to give great impact, strength and durability, with the extremely low absorption that is required in public eating places. Decorations are applied between the body and the glaze, thereby protecting the decoration during commercial use.

Most of the ware is subject to a high-temperature first firing, and low-temperature second firing. Some ware is fired, however, in a one-fire operation wherein the body and glaze mature at the same time. Like fine china, American restaurant china is vitrified.

Run of Kiln (or R. K.) - a grading term denoting dinnerware as it comes out of the kiln, not subjected to inspection or weeding out.

Saggers - fire-resistant containers for articles to be fired.

Salt glaze - a semi-mat or half-glossy glaze obtained by injecting salt into the kiln during the glaze firing.

Screen printing - a method of ceramic and glassware decorating in which stencil-like screens are used in applying colors to the ware.

Seam - a ridge on a piece of molded hollow ware caused by the tiny crack between two or more parts of the mold.

Seconds - in the vernacular of the consumer, ware with slight defects, frequently not even detectable, offered at prices below what they would ordinarily have to pay for so-called perfect ware.

Selection - the weeding out of imperfect ware, a process to which dinnerware is subjected at various stages in its manufacture.

Selects - near-perfect dinnerware pieces as determined by careful inspection and removal from the group of imperfect pieces.

Semi-vitrified (or semi-porcelain) - a type of dinnerware about halfway between china and earthenware in appearance and durability.

Sgraffito - a type of ceramic decoration produced by coating a piece with a layer of colored slip, or liquid clay, then incising a design in that layer to let the original body color show through.

Shoulder - the raised rim of a traditionally-shaped plate.

Silica - one of the earth's most abundant minerals and a vital ingredient in ceramic manufacture. It is the basic component of glass as well as of ceramic glazes and high-quality clay ware bodies.

Slip - clay mixed with water to a creamy consistency.

Slip coating - a layer of slip applied to a clay ware body for decorative effect.

Stoneware - a non-porous ceramic body made of unprocessed clays, or of clay and flux additives, fired at elevated temperatures. It is quite durable but lacks the translucence and whiteness of china. It is resistant to chipping and rings clearly when struck. It differs from porcelain chiefly in that it is colored rather than white, which results from iron or other impurities in the clay.

Tank - a furnace used in the glass manufacturing process, the walls of which are of refractory brick that serves to retain the heat and hold the molten glass.

Terra cotta - a hard, unglazed earthenware used most frequently for vases and architectural decoration.

Texture glaze - a colored glaze in which dripping, running, eruption, or some other controlled disturbance is introduced to heighten the decorative effect.

Toby jug - a small jug or mug in the form of a stout old man wearing a three-cornered hat that serves as the mouth of the vessel.

Torte plate - a glass serving plate for sandwiches, cake, or cold meat. Comparable to a chop plate in dinnerware, it ranges in size from about 12 to 20 inches.

Transfer printing - a decorating method similar to the one in which decalcomania is used but permitting only one color at a time to be applied.

Translucence - that quality of fine china or plastic dinnerware that makes it semi-transparent. It may be demonstrated by placing the hand across the back of a piece and holding it up to the light. A silhouette of the hand will be visible through the body of the piece.

Tunnel kiln - a long, tunnel-like oven in which dinnerware is fired as it moves through on slow-moving flat cars.

Underglaze decoration - a ceramic decoration that is applied directly to the biscuit, or unglazed body, and then covered with a protective glaze coating that makes it highly resistant to wear.

The terms **vitrified, vitreous** and **semivitreous** describe the relative openness of the fired ceramic body. This openness is determined by immersing a piece of unglazed ware in water under specific conditions and determining the amount of water absorbed into the open pores of the body. By Federal government standards, a body gaining less than 0.5%, by weight, is termed vitrified or vitreous; a body with more open pores is termed semivitreous. The terms absorption and porosity are more or less synonomous, with the former referring to the relative volume of water added to the open pores and the latter referring to the relative volume of water added to the pores. Vitrification is brought about by the temperature and time of firing as well as by the amount and type of fluxing agents added to the composition.

Wasters - pieces marred in the kiln.

Index

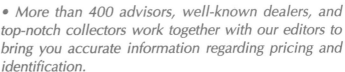